MOUNTAINBIKE SCOTLAND

THE HIGHLANDS
by Kenny Wilson

WWW.MOUNTAINBIKESCOTLAND.COM

II

First published by The Ernest press 2006
Copyright © Kenny Wilson 2006

ISBN 0 948153 81 4
British Library Cataloguing-in-Publication Data has been registered with the British Library and is available on request

Disclaimer:
The author and publisher have made every effort to ensure that the information contained in this publication is accurate.

The author and publisher accept no responsibility for any loss, injury, inconvenience occasioned by any person using the information contained within this publication or of damage to or infringement of the rights of others resulting from improper use of any such information.

Mountain biking is an adventure sport and has associated risks that must be identified and accepted by all who choose to pursue it.

No right to access to the countryside is inferred beyond anything conferred by current legislation.

Maps within this publication are not to scale and are intended to serve illustrative purposes only.

CONTENTS

IV

ACKNOWLEDGEMENTS

I'd like to thank everyone who assisted in the preparation of this book. Many have helped with advice, content, photos and just being there on the days spent riding. So, a special thanks to Sunny Dunny, MACEWAN, Crispin, Steve B, IPV, Christel, Billy, Eddie, Gary, Fergal, Marko and all the muppets from Stirling Bike Club (SBC).

Added to the list must be David of bothy Bikes in Aviemore, Lindsay of Basecamp MTB at Laggan Wolftrax, Paul from Mid-Argyll CC, Niall Thompson from the Carron Valley Project (CVP), Richard Barton of the CVP & IMBA UK and the Ecurie Neep CC.

The deepest thanks must go to my immediate family. Without the support of Patti & the boys I'd be lost. This book has been the least of it!

FOREWORD

In 2004 Britain's most popular mountain biking magazine, Mountain Bike rider (MBR) gave away a free CD to its readers. It was entitled 'The 50 best MBR pictures ever'. The images ranged from riding in the US, Europe and beyond. It is no coincidence that nine of the total were pictures of Scottish riding.

Scotland is a mountain biking paradise. The World Cup events held at the Nevis Range have been voted the best on the calendar. The prepared pistes at the purpose-built centres are second to none and have received similar recognition. For several years, the International Mountain Bicycling Association (IMBA) judged them as the best in Europe. This was quite an achievement and all thanks to the work and planning of those who had the vision and the ability to make it happen. In 2006 the IMBA voted Scotland the best mountain biking destination in the world. It's great news for the country in general and the sport in particular.

What have yet to see full recognition are Scotland's biggest assets as a world class mountain biking destination. The landscape and the fabulous wilderness mountain biking to be experienced within it are fantastic! Off the beaten track there are thousands of kilometres of superb trails that lie waiting for you to visit. Taken together with the man made trails, they make Scotland a place that no mountainbiker should miss.

While this book will make reference to a number of the riding centres they are present as bad weather alternatives in addition to being great places to ride in their own right. Instead the book focuses on wilderness trails that will challenge and delight every kind of rider.

Although, nominally, there are fifty routes presented the number of days riding far exceeds that total. Multi day routes and the variations highlighted ensure that the content will keep even the most avid rider going for a long time to come.

Some trips are established classics that have stood the test of time. Others are well known to enthusiasts but will be making their first appearance in print within these pages. Plenty will be totally new to all but the few who have explored their possibilities for themselves. All are fabulous days with an extraordinary variety of riding through some of the best of our scenery. Together they will help you savour your bike and the Highlands to the utmost.

Unfortunately, it's only possible to bring a fraction of what's out there. Some have been left out because they have delicate sections that should not see the extra traffic generated by inclusion in a guide. Others are absent because of oaths of secrecy. Yet more have been set aside simply because something has to be left for the explorer that lies in all of us.

HIGHLAND AREA ROADS

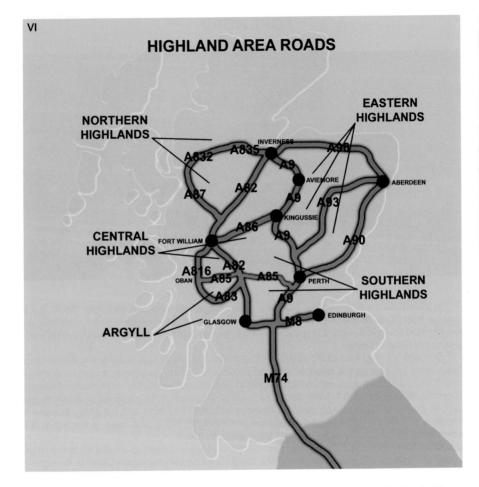

The map above supplies an overview of the main road routes through the Highlands. There are many more but those shown offer the easiest travel between the routes included in this book. Where other roads are necessary they will be mentioned in the text for the relevant route. Also an area map is provided for each section showing the main roads to help travel through them.

One thing that is worth bearing in mind is that the Scottish weather is dominated by warm moist air arriving from the Atlantic. Because of this, the climate differs substantially from West to East with the East being a bit drier. If the weather is bad near one coast it is often possible to enjoy sunshine in the hills on the opposite side. For that reason the A86 is a valuable link between the two. Much excellent wilderness riding can be reached from it as well as the centres of Nevis range and Laggan Wolf Trax.

Anyone coming to the country for any outdoor sports, not just mountain biking, could do worse than consider Kingussie, or its near neighbour Newtonmore, as a base from which all other areas are most easily reached.

BIKE SHOPS IN THE HIGHLANDS

If you're in the Highlands and you find you've forgotten anything from inner tubes to eye wear you'll want to know where to get some. The list below is not comprehensive but they are the best placed to serve the needs of anyone moving around the routes in the book.

They're all shops that specialise in mountain biking kit and run or staffed by enthusiasts. You'll be able to get far more than the sundries mentioned above.

The sport is followed by a huge number of people who live near these outlets. The local riders are experienced and discerning. So, don't think for one moment that the shops are any less sophisticated than those you'd expect in the average city high street. If anything you'll be more likely to find the stuff that actually does the job!

Many of the shops offer just that little bit more and have a wealth of knowledge on the local trails that they are willing to share. If you're in their area they're worth a visit.

ARGYLL
Crinan Cycles, 34 Argyll St. Lochgilphead, 01546 603511
Bike hire
SOUTHERN HIGHLANDS
Trossachs Cycles, off the A81 S of Aberfoyle, 01877 382614
Bike hire, Accommodation
www.trossachsholidays.co.uk
Wheels Cycling Centre, Invertrossachs Rd, by Callander, 01877 33100
Bike Hire, Bike Wash, Accommodation
www.scottish-cycling.com
Escape Route, 3 Athol Rd, Pitlochry, 01796 473859
Bike Hire
www.escape-route.biz
CENTRAL HIGHLANDS
Offbeat Bikes, High St. Fort William, 01397 704008
Bike Hire, with full suspension rigs + armour + lift pass packages available for the DH course at Aonach Mor
www.offbeatbikes.co.uk
Nevis Cycles, 4 Lochy Crescent, Inverlochy, by Fort William, 01397 705555
Bike Hire, Bike and rider shuttle by arrangement
www.neviscycles.com
Basecamp MTB, Laggan Wolf Trax, Strathmashie by Newtonmore, 01528 5447786
Bike hire, Bike Wash, Bike Shuttle to top of runs
www.basecampmtb.com
Eastern Highlands
Bothy Bikes, Grampian Road, Inverdruie, by Aviemore, 01479 810111
Bike Hire, Evening rides from shop
www.bothybikes.co.uk
Fat Tread Bikes, Unit 9, Myrtlefield Shopping Centre, Aviemore, 01479 812019
www.fattreadbikes.co.uk
Northern Highlands
Highland Cycles, 16a Telford St, Inverness, 01463 234789
Local rides from shop
www.highlandbikes.com
Square Wheels, The Square, Strathpeffer, 01997 421000
www.squarewheels.biz

BIKES & BITS

Since this is a 'where to' as opposed to a 'how to' book there's no sense in dwelling too much on the subject of bikes. It's likely that you'll already have one. Nevertheless, if you're agonising over whether your own will be up to the demands of some of the rides there's probably nothing to worry about. A well fitting and properly maintained bike is far more important than the latest all singing - all dancing machine.

Strictly speaking suspension isn't really a must. Each and every wilderness route contained in this book has been ridden on fully rigid bikes. While that approach would not be the choice of most of us, it's proof that the most important piece of equipment on any day is the rider.

The exception might be a really cheap bike such as those bought from high street catalogue shops. Just remember the old adage "Buy cheap....buy twice!"

Should you be on the lookout for a new bike or upgrades to your current steed then the first port of call should really be your local bike shop. Unless you are an expert mechanic, with all the necessary tools, you will eventually need to call on their services. If you've bought all your kit on the internet you'll have saved money but find yourself at the back of the queue as a result.

Further advice can be had from mountain bike specific magazines. You'll not go wrong with any of the following, Mountain Bike Rider (MBR), What Mountain Bike (WMB) and Singletrack. Singletrack also has an excellent website with a very active forum where all your questions on any aspect of mountain biking will find loads of folk ready to answer them. You'll be able to meet them @ www.singletrackworld.com.

Another handy site is Bike Magic @ www.bikemagic.com. For mainly route information you could try Offroad Adventures @ www.offroadadventures-online.com.

The most active Scottish site is that of Stirling Bike Club. You will be able to log into it @ www.stirlingbikeclub.org.uk . There's a genuine friendliness and depth of knowledge of the Scottish Riding scene waiting there.

With all this readily available information, it's a bit redundant to recommend any specific equipment. What has to be suggested is that if you are considering replacement forks, hubs, headsets, handlebars, stems etc. it makes sense to get stuff that's robust, easily serviced and widely available. Also important is that it should be designed and built for British riding conditions. All of these criteria are met by the products made by Pace, Hope, USE and Middleburn. The same can be said of clothing by the Scottish firm Endura who make superb kit that lasts when all others have disintegrated. I have yet to ride with any serious mountain biker who does not own at least some kit from the above names.

In terms of bike clothing it is assumed that you will wear and carry appropriate protection from the elements. This means proper cycling shorts worn next to the skin and sufficient layers to respond to the changeable conditions that are a feature of our climate.

Helmet, eye protection and cycling gloves (or mitts) should be worn at all times. Additional protection in the form of arm and leg armour should be worn on serious ground. They may be bulky and inconvenient but there are few inconveniences like a chipped humerus or patella (in the middle of nowhere) to make you wish you'd worn them.

The mention of injury brings 1st aid to the fore. You're pursuing an adventure activity in the great outdoors. Injury is something that goes hand in hand with that. Carry a decent 1st aid kit and know how to administer primary care.

It's not only people who get injured, your poor old bike takes a pounding and even the best engineered kit needs to be looked after. You should know how to fix punctures, mend tyre side walls, true wheels, fix/adjust the drivetrain, brakes and steering. This knowledge will make sure that the bike remains an aid rather than an encumbrance. Of course, you'll need the appropriate tools and spares with you as well as sufficient food and water to see you through the day.

Lastly, get yourself a decent sized hydration pack to put all this stuff in. Forget the wee slimline efforts that struggle to accommodate a rolled up hankie. Space left unused is infinitely more desirable than leaving a vital item behind because it wouldn't fit.

Please make sure you are well prepared for most eventualities as some of the routes in this book take you a long way from anywhere.

USING THE GUIDE

The whole point of this book is to provide the information necessary to gain access to the great mountain biking throughout the Highlands. Trails for every grade of rider have been included. The beginner will be able to progress through the easier routes picking up fitness and skill along the way. The more experienced will have a choices to test ability and stamina. All the routes described are first class outings. In the process of working your way through them, trails of the best quality will be ridden and places visited that might, otherwise, have been missed.

However, it's no just about mountain biking. In the Highlands, travelling from point to point is always a pleasure. No matter how many times any journey is repeated the time of day, the season or the quality of light is likely to have changed. These variables can transform even the most mundane scene into one of staggering beauty. This happy circumstance means that the scenery getting to and from the routes will often be spectacular. But, seldom as stunning as that on the rides themselves.

Those who do not venture into the hills cannot fully experience their true character and changes of mood. Making sure you get to see some of this at first hand was pivotal in what has been included. Many of the routes will take you to astounding places and leave you hungry for more. However, it *is* the riding that remains the main focus.

The way any mountain biking trip fits together is of great importance and can make or break it in the quality stakes. We've tried to ensure the itineraries are as varied as possible and reflect the character of the areas through which they pass. The routes are mainly singletrack rich and, depending on the rider, such days provide anything from romps to challenging expeditions. They can be tackled according to fitness, ability mood and conditions. Where a route is confined to landrover tracks it will always offer stunning views and reliable riding surfaces with exciting descents. The appeal of these outings goes beyond simply catering for beginners and they remain worthwhile trips for any rider.

Regardless of their type, many of the routes can be started from a variety of places. The start points and directions of travel quoted probably represent the optimum but most can be tackled in the opposite direction from the one suggested in the texts.

Choice also applies to routes where alternative paths could be taken. Some of these have been shown on the maps that accompany the route descriptions and reflect that this is a guide and not a text book. The options are there for you to explore and allow the possibility of variation of any of the days.

What has to be said is that, wherever possible, we've tried to ensure that there's a bit of reasonably gentle pedalling to warm the legs up before any real hard work begins and the riding livens up. Often the action continues right up to the end of the day and you'll arrive back at the start point still buzzing.

In the following pages, we have included an explanation of how the route information is presented and a bit of guidance on where your current riding level might fit into the picture.

Route Title

The name given to each day usually reflects its location. Sometimes this will be obvious and refer to the main glen it travels through or the mountains or lochs that are prominent on the trip.   In some instances a route will have acquired a name, over time, like the Leacann Muir and Burma Roads, we have stayed with these. A few refer to significant or notorious bits of the days' riding such as the "Ciaran Path" or "Bealach an Sgairne".

Beneath each route title is the number of the Ordnance Survey 1:50,000 Landranger series map or maps on which they appear. The appropriate Ordnance Survey map should always be carried.

Distance

A rough guide to within a Kor so of the day's total. Speaks for itself really doesn't it?

Ascent

Total height gained and, don't forget, descent which follows (Tip : Learn to love climbing!)

Skill

Four simple to understand subjective grades that correspond roughly to the colour coded system used in skiing and now being adopted at riding centres

Easy

Ordinary, sound bike handling skills.

Intermediate

Enhanced skills in braking, cornering and weighting/unweighting wheels.

Advanced

Trails with a variety of obstacles requiring the exercise of some technical skills

Includes steep climbing/descending, front & rear wheel lifts and moderate drops in a variety of conditions and on variable trail surfaces.

Expert

Only for those who possess a full range of handling skills allied to the strength, fitness and confidence to tackle sizeable trail obstacles.

Overall

Length and total height gain are not the only factors in the demands a route will make on the rider. Steepness, roughness and many other factors affect the amount of effort a route requires.

Moderate

Should be do able by any person of moderate fitness who rides regularly.

Challenging

Longer or steeper days that may stretch those who have yet to toughen up.

Hard

Usually long, demanding, days that require strength and stamina.

Epic

Serious days for those with the resilience to keep going when other peoples' tanks are empty.

Getting there

Road, rail and other travel directions.

Route text

In this part of the information we have attempted to bring a little of the flavour of each of the rides and presented it in a manner we hope will inspire you to get out and tackle them.

Significant trail hazards will be highlighted ; in particular river crossings.

Directions

Invariably you will be following linear features. Regardless of this aspect attention must always be paid as it can be easy to miss a turning point.

There are only a few occasions where the trail to be followed becomes indistinct. These are highlighted and appropriate instruction included to regain the continuation.

Each route has a number of way points and these are numbered. They are described and an Ordnance Survey grid reference quoted.

In the depiction of the trail that lies between each waypoint the following abbreviations are used.

SA = straight ahead

R = Right and L = Left in relation to direction of travel.

N,S,E & W refer to points of the compass.

Junct = junction

LRT = Landrover track

Map

Our maps are intended only to show how any route fits into its landscape and each is to a slightly different scale.

Due to the limited space available, differences in scale and shape of each route, a number of maps have not been orientated with North to the top of the page.

Please check each map to see which way N lies.

Except for the very simplest of days, the Ordnance Survey map for the route should be used.

You should have the ability to use the map and the compass necessary for proper navigational technique.

The key at the foot of the page highlights the different types of linear feature that appear on the maps.

NB A conscious decision has been taken not to include a time estimate for each route. This is such a moveable feast as to be a relatively meaningless statistic. It depends on fitness, conditions, party size, number of punctures or maintenance stops, photographs taken or whether you want to just loaf about and enjoy the whole experience. Individuals and groups will, by dint of experience, have a good idea of their average speed on different types of terrain.

Riders venturing into the mountains must acquire a number of methods of establishing their location at any time during a ride, all are valid. No single one, except traditional map and compass work, should be relied upon to the exclusion of any other.

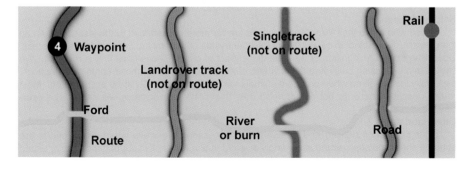

ACCESS

For many years a *de facto* right to roam existed in Scotland through a *modus vivendi* enjoyed between walkers and land owners. Translated from the gobbledygook that meant there wasn't actually much of a problem. Officially, cyclists were allowed to ride rights of way provided these had seen a history of being ridden without objection. In practical terms, there was little trouble riding a bike anywhere. However, some landowners and managers were not so keen. Their personal experiences of members of the mountain biking fraternity, who were less than careful, left them with a jaundiced view of the sport. Changes in legislation mean that things have moved on a bit and the interests of everyone have been addressed. Also, improvements in bikes means that they are much more controllable and reliable.

In 2005 access to the Scottish countryside was formalised in law. The legislation included cycling within its scope but not without conditions. Rightly, the needs of those who live and work in the countryside have been taken into account, along with the environment in general. In conferring these rights, the Scottish Outdoor Access Code emphasises responsibility in exercising them. You can look at the code in detail @ www.outdooraccess-scotland.com.

Also, Scottish Natural Heritage published a leaflet entitled 'Know the Code.' It contains the following guidance.

"Access rights come with responsibilities, which are fully explained in the Scottish Outdoor Access Code, though the main thing is to use common sense. You need to take responsibility for your own actions, respect the interests of others and care for the environment - what does this mean?"

The leaflet asks you to take responsibility for your own actions, respect other people's privacy and peace of mind, help farmers, landowners and others to work safely and effectively and to care for the environment. The advice contained is sound but it wouldn't be correct to publish this book without some direct address of the issue.

Responsibility

The majority of us enjoy the thrill of speed and technical challenge. In the process we often scare ourselves witless. Those who do not ride have little knowledge that a rider hurtling downhill will most likely be exerting a great deal of control. Often the interpretation of the non-cyclist is one of impending danger. To help avoid this upset, wait until a descent is clear or ride it in such a manner that no such threat is perceived. If there are blind bends or dips and the conditions are right to ride it flat out, send a spotter ahead, to make sure the way is clear. Due consideration should always be given to livestock and wildlife in this regard as well.

Respect for privacy

You should not enter people's private gardens or go too close to homes. On occasions a track might pass through farm buildings that might include people's houses. Be on the alert for, and ready to use, alternatives provided near such buildings.

Helping farmers

Those who make their living from the land are far more accustomed to the issues thrown up than we are. Few object to casual use of the countryside and many are proud to facilitate access. Observing simple recognition of the potential impact of our presence is all that is required. We should avoid crossing cultivated fields where crops are growing and those containing livestock, especially in springtime when pregnant animals and newborn are likely to be encountered. Most routes described here do not compromise this. Nevertheless, vigilance will need to be exercised.

Other land users

During the deer stalking and grouse shooting seasons the areas where these sports are pursued should be approached accordingly or avoided altogether. If in doubt the particular estate should be consulted and guidance sought and complied with. Regardless of your own feelings on blood sports they are an integral feature of country life. Many of the tracks and trails followed would simply not exist if it were not for their roles in such activities. Always be on the lookout for the presence of any other operation on cultivated land or forests where your presence might interfere. If in doubt seek advice according to the situation. These precautions are as much for your own safety as anything else.

Caring for the environment

This is perhaps the biggest issue affecting wilderness riding. There can be no argument against the proposition that *every* form of land use causes erosion. However, there is little profit in pursuing the oft-quoted fact that much damage takes place where no bike has ever been. This will never change the truth that an unsympathetically ridden bike will cause significant damage.

Skidding in particular will cut a gouge in any unhardened surface. Such damage will be worsened by the next significant rainfall.

Any rider on a vulnerable surface should have the skill to stop without locking their wheels and the self-discipline to remain within the parameters that allow this. This applies equally to descending or "spinning out" on ascents. It will vary according to the ground encountered and the abilities of the rider concerned. No route described here, outside the riding centres, should be tackled without taking these factors into account.

Even in the riding centres much damage is caused by those who insist on carrying too much speed into corners or up to trail ends. The harsh braking that is then performed results in braking bumps. These require constant attention and maintenance due to damage that is needlessly caused. If in doubt, get off and walk!

Where a trail exists stick to it! On some trails sharp corners will be encountered. These might prevent those without enough skill from negotiating them successfully. Either acquire the ability to lift your rear wheel while moving, and steering with the front, or get off and walk. Under no circumstance should corners be cut as new erosion will be started.

Boggy sections of trail should not be worsened. At all costs the tactic of riding round them must be avoided, this will simply broaden the problem area. Straight through, wet bum and all, is normally the correct thing to do. The option of dismounting should also be considered. The same option should also be borne in mind on the rare occasions where no actual defined path exists. On some routes this kind of ground will be met. It appears most often at the watersheds traversed in passing from one glen to the next. In dry or frozen conditions such terrain may be ridden with minimal impact. If it is soft and the wheels begin to sink into it, even slightly, walk.

All of the above problems are lessened, not cured, by the use of large volume tyres. These give more control in descent, provide better traction in ascent and go some way to spreading weight on soft ground. Narrow profile tyres, billed as being specifically for muddy conditions, are designed to cut through the soft upper surface and search for traction beneath it. They have little or no place in wilderness riding. In any case the design of many of them makes their use on rocky surfaces or road sections dangerous for the rider.

Wildlife

In general, mountainbikers follow well defined linear routes. More often than not the furred and feathered wild things will be aware of you long before you get anywhere near them. One exception is their young. Often it takes a wee while for young animals to develop their full range of survival instincts. From time to time restrictions may be met due to breeding populations, particularly birds. Please comply willingly with these. There is always the temptation to say to yourself "It's only me/us" what might be missed is that someone might have been there five minutes before with the same idea. Then, five minutes later, someone does the same thing. Get the picture? If restrictions are in place please rethink your route. There are plenty of alternatives to choose from in this book.

Litter

It might seem redundant to mention litter but a look round any of the riding centres will see significant amounts of this menace in places where no walkers ever go. Please make sure the likes of snack wrappers, dead inner tubes and replaced gear/brake cables are carried home.

General

For many, who cherish the countryside, access has always been regarded as a privilege. Despite the existence of any legislation it's a frame of mind that has much to commend it.

Finally, the International mountain bicycling Association (IMBA) works for socially acceptable and environmentally sustainable riding. Kind of sums the whole thing up doesn't it? You can find out what they're all about @ www.imba.co.uk

PHOTOGRAPHS

The photographs listed below were supplied and kind permission granted by the following.

Lairig Leacach (p122) & Abhainn Rath (p 54) Niall Thompson collection.
Devil's Staircase (p52) Eddie Addis collection.
Swampthing entry (p21) Mid Argyll CC
Wolf Trax pictures (p 60 & 61)Basecamp MTB

The bulk of the remainder of the pictures were all taken 'on the run' on a 2.1 mega pixel compact digital camera kept in a padded case attached to the waist belt my hydration pack.

Contrary to popular myth, the sun does shine in Scotland. Hopefully some of the pictures might have a few more people actually believing it.

If you like any of the pictures and fancy them as wallpaper for your PC you can download some of them (free) by visiting www.mountainbikescotland.com

Argyll singletrack

ARGYLL AREA MAP

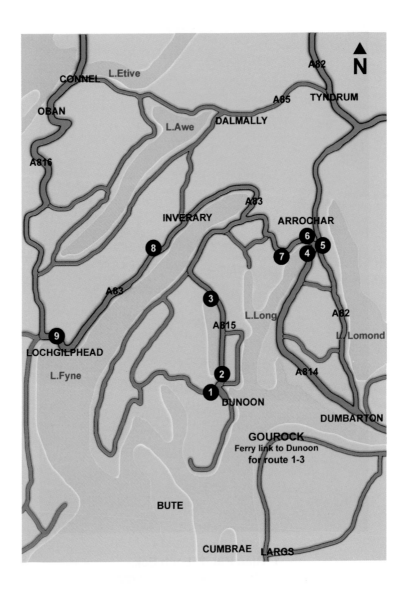

Dominated by its two main features, steep rugged hills and fjord-like lochs Argyll is one of the most mountainous regions in the country. The mixture is very distinct and makes for a unique feel that is not seen elsewhere in the British Isles. Unfortunately, the heads of many of the glens end in trackless boggy wildernesses. Although these places are wild and inspiring they seldom present through routes for all but the most determined biker. Exceptions do exist and the routes presented here provide the best ways through the county's mountains. Their positions are shown on the map opposite.

Starting in the South, the Glen Kin route is an easy intro to the area and to mountain biking itself. It can be easily linked to its near neighbour, the Loch Eck circuit. That route provides a magnificent tour round a truly beautiful body of water. The shortish day at the head of the loch, the Glen Branter route, is a gem that stands up well on its own but woven into a big day with Loch Eck helps make a superb tour that nudges toward the epic.

Moving round to route four, the sortie up Glen Douglas gives the rider of modest ability a chance to taste some thrills and brilliant elevated views of Lochs Lomond and Long in a day that can be broken up with plenty of stops. Likewise the 'Bonny Banks' route visits the shores of Loch Lomond but provides a sterner test in distance covered, height climbed and technical difficulty. It uses the ferries on the loch to complete a truly unique riding experience. The Coiregrogain and Ardgartan circuits can be done separately or linked together to make trips that penetrate deep into the corries of the Arrochar Alps. In the process, they provide exciting riding and stunning views of the surrounding hills.

The main event in the area is the 'Leacann Muir Road'. It's a true test of skill and endurance for experienced riders. The sign in the picture above will be met on it and points the way to the delights of its closing section. It's a stunner of a route that shouldn't be missed. Finally, the riding round Lochgilphead on the Mid-Argyll Trails is supplemented by the excellent Fire Tower trail, a dedicated, man-made, cycle trail that provides year round excitement on tracks built by riders for riders. As well as providing a great bolt-hole in poor weather it's a worthwhile destination on its own.

GLEN KIN
Landranger Sheet 56
Distance : 10K Ascent : 300m
Skills : Easy   Overall : Moderate
Getting there : From the S M8, or train to Gourock then ferry to Dunoon.
From the N A83

This little circuit provides a sheltered and scenic loop that will entertain any rider. In its basic form it travels round a typical small Scottish glen and lets you enjoy a couple of straightforward speedy descents that will bring a smile to your face.

The real beauty of the riding here is that there are easily found alternatives where you will be able to practise your skills. These optional trails are not marked on the Landranger series maps but are easy enough to locate. Two are marked on the map opposite and there are a couple of others. If you look you will find them.

In addition to the singletrack shown in the picture above (the link on the E side of the glen) there are steep descents, tough climbs and technical root-strewn sections to test the most able on other parts of the alternatives. Following any of the available variations increases the difficulty considerably. Portions of them were formerly used in Scottish Cyclist's Union cross country races.

It's a fun place to ride in its own right and, for fit riders, makes a great start to route 2. A link to that route can be made from the entry to the LRT just uphill from the start of this one.

1. Parking at side of B836 at bridge over Glen Kin Burn, grid ref 133814 : Head up track on W side of glen to **2. Junction at 132806 :** Turn L and climb to **3. Junction, grid ref. 141805 :** turn R & follow main track round glen to return to B836

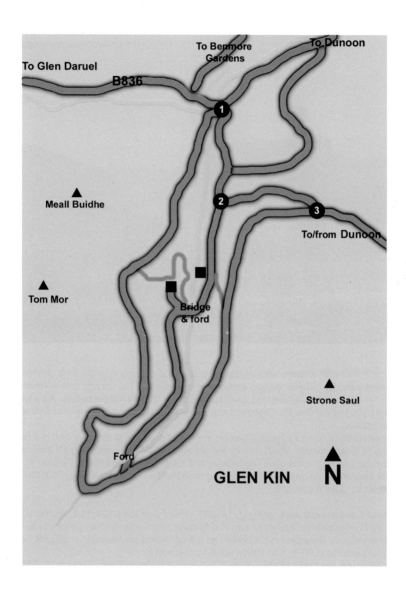

LOCH ECK
Map OS Landranger Sheet 56
Distance : 35K   Ascent : 1,400m
Skill : Easy/ Intermediate   Overall : Challenging
Getting there : From Glasgow M8, or train, to Gourock + ferry to Dunoon. From N A83

A superb route for anyone wanting to enjoy stunning scenery and physical challenge without technical difficulty. There are two sections of singletrack. The second one is steep and will provide a test of your slow speed cornering technique on its tight hairpin bends. As a whole, the route takes you high above the beautiful Loch Eck and offers many fine viewpoints that allow it to be appreciated.

With all-weather riding surfaces it can be tackled at any time of the year and is a rewarding trip for any standard of rider. Watch out for the big climb on the homeward leg it's a monster! The reward for completing it is the view seen above and the rushing descents that follow.

Taken as a whole the day is a fabulous expedition that can be extended into Glen Shellish and Glen Branter to make a true epic.

1. Benmore Gardens car park, grid ref. 143855 : Head over the bridge to **2. Surfaced private road** : turn R ride past clock tower to turn R & N toward the Loch, tarmac gives way to LRT at a gate, follow this to **3. Gate grid ref. 134918** : go L & uphill and stay on main track until it dwindles to ST and an exit onto LRT to turn L then uphill to descend to

4. Track junction, grid ref 111969 : Turn R & descend to Glenbranter village to **5. A815** : Turn R and continue past the Lauder memorial to **6. Entry to LRT on L , grid ref. 122975** : begin *the* climb, up the zigzags to the high track that heads S above the loch & follow it to descents and exit at **7. Road to Ardentinny, grid ref. 150924** : Straight over the road and into track system to take 1st R toward the loch and the track that heads S toward the start, at a gate, below Creag Liath, it becomes ST, climb then descend to **8. Exit to A815** : Turn L and cover the short distance to the start.

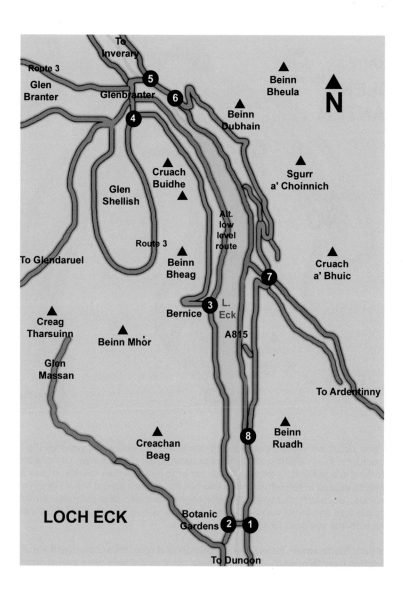

GLEN BRANTER
Map OS Landranger Sheet 56
Distance : 18K Ascent : 520m
Skills : Easy   Overall : Moderate
Getting there : From Glasgow M8 or train, to Gourock + ferry to Dunoon. From N A83

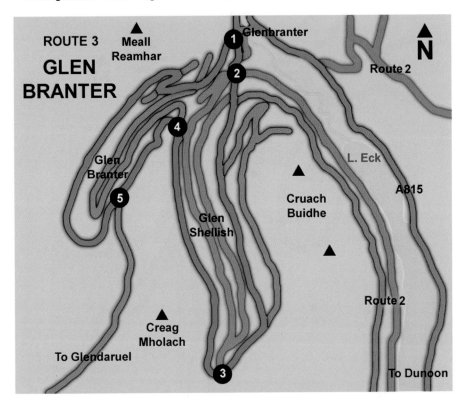

This wee circuit will probably appeal to those looking to extend the previous trip but it's a pleasant outing in itself. Starting at the forestry commission car park near Glenbranter village, the whole thing is a straightforward loop that is easier to navigate than the map makes it appear.

It's easy to exceed 50kph without much effort on the descent toward 4 and 70kph on the last, steep sections. So, watch your speed and look out for foot traffic, especially near the end where the bends are tight and forest walks join/leave the route. Good surface, rideable all year round. Just make sure that you don't turn off at 5!

1. FC car park Glenbranter : Head out of the car park and down toward the river & turn R to climb to **2. Junction near farm grid ref. 111973 :** head uphill on a steady climb then short descent to **3. Junction, grid ref 109930 :** Ignore R turn and climb to point where long fast descent passes 1 junct. to **4. Junction , grid ref 103966 :** Possible esc. to lower route on R but keep dead ahead to **5. Junction, grid ref 094955 :** Descend a little then another climb round glen, screaming descent round zig zags begins after mature trees are reached. Beware walkers and gate at bottom.

Map OS Landranger Sheet 56
Distance : 24K Ascent : 700m
Skills : Easy Overall : Moderate/Challenging
Getting there : From the S A82, via Dumbarton. From the N A82 via Crianlarich or A83

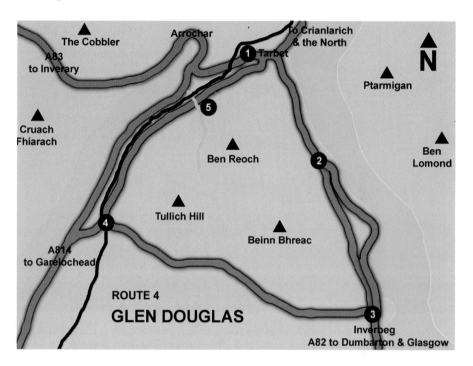

If easy off-road riding, and simple navigation, accompanied by classic views of Ben Lomond and the Arrochar Alps are what you're in the mood for then this route should fit the bill.

The opening section is a gentle amble along Loch Lomondside using the cycle path to take you to Inverbeg. Part of the payback starts at this spot with the climb up Glen Douglas. Once the price of the climb is paid, you are rewarded with the vista on the opposite side of Loch long. You now also have access to some fun riding along the landrover track that heads in the general direction of Tarbet. While on this you will pay the second price for your pleasure when you cross the An-t-Sreang (string) burn. Your feet will get wet but there's not far to go. Although it's deep it's safe in all but the heaviest of conditions. Just shoulder the bike and go for it.

A short leg takes you back to the A83 and a return to the start where a cuppa and buns can be enjoyed at the café near the station after a first class bike run.

1. Tarbet Railway Station : Head for Loch Lomond, turn R and head S to **2. Entry to Cycle Path, grid ref. 327025 :** follow the cycle path, with its many viewpoints, to **3. Inverbeg :** Head up Glen Douglas road **4. Exit onto track on R at 274002 :** Head along track for traversing descent with great views over to Arrochar Alps to **5. Crossing of the Ant-Sreang :** Sometimes deep (traverse of pipe at side not recommended) scrabble down to the watercourse, through it, and up opposite bank to continuation of track & return to Tarbet

THE BONNY BANKS
Map OS Landranger Sheet 56
Distance : 33K (3 by boat!) Ascent : 1,000m
Skill : Intermediate/ Advanced   Overall : Hard
Getting there : from the S A82, from the N A82 or A83

The old song proclaims the virtues of 'the bonny, bonny banks of Loch Lomond' and it's not wrong. The scenery around the loch is stunning. This route provides riding to match. It does so, on each of the banks, using ferries run by the Rowerdennan and Inversnaid hotels. These are seasonal and weather dependent. So, check their availability before setting out. However, they give unique views of the loch and 'The Ben' that you might not otherwise get. They also bring an unusual dimension to a bike ride.

Having mentioned the song, it would be wrong not to include 'high road' and 'low road' options. The choices highlighted allow you to adjust the route according to time, taste and energy levels. It's a superb day out and one that should be on every mountain biker's 'To Do' list, regardless of ability levels.

1. Tarbet Railway Station : Head for Loch Lomond, turn R and head S to **2. Entry to Cycle Path, grid ref. 327025 :** follow the cycle path, with its many viewpoints, to **3. Inverbeg : take** ferry to **4. Rowardennan :** head N along WHW (high road or low) to **5. Inversnaid :** Take ferry to **6. Inveruglas :** Cross A82, turn L, and take path to **7. Loch Sloy Access Road :** Head uphill, under railway, to **8. Junction With Road to Ardvorlich, grid ref. 310093 :** Carry straight on to **9. L Turn to Bridge, grid ref. 303092:** Descend to bridge and follow ST (see Coiregrogain route for details) to **10. Path Junction, grid ref 301052 :** take L fork and follow path system to Tarbet (high road) or R to Arrochar and return by road (low).

Variation : N from Inveruglas on A82 to turn off at Ardvorlich grid ref. 325120 (7a on map)
For Ferries Rowardennan Hotel 01360870273   Invesrnaid Hotel   01877386223

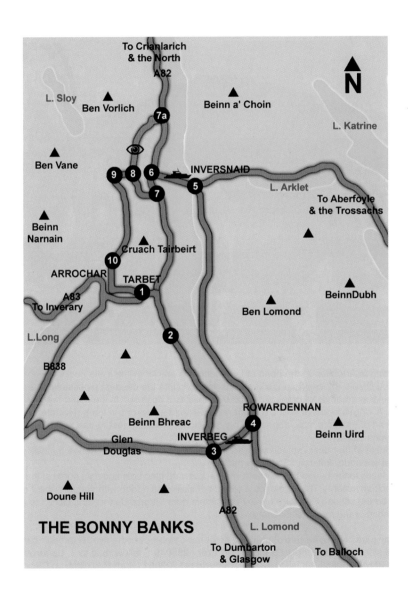

COIRE GROGAIN
Map OS Landranger Sheet 56
Distance : 18K   Ascent : 580m
Skill : Intermediate/ Advanced   Overall : Moderate/Hard
Getting there : From L. Lomond (S or N) A82 then A83 , from the N A83

Starting in Arrochar, at the head of Loch long this cracking little route packs a whole lot into a tiny wee circuit. In less than 20k it carries you high into the deepest recesses of the Arrochar Alps providing great views of the surrounding peaks as it does so. In the upper reaches of Coire Grogain, A' Chrois looms at your L shoulder and Beinn Ime beckons in front. The stream crossing at the head of the coire may, depending on conditions, provide a test for the skilled and wet feet for everyone else.

A couple of fast descents follow. The first has many sharp-edged stones that will puncture tyres that are under-inflated. So be warned.

It all leads to the bridge that will take you back toward glen Loin and onto some of the loveliest singletrack anywhere. This demands a wee bit of skill to be ridden with the panache it deserves but can be descended with care by any competent rider. It provides a fitting climax to a superb route among grand mountain scenery.

1. FC car park, opposite petrol station, Arrochar : Head over the river & through car park on opposite side to **2. Turn off to Succoth grid ref. 295049 :** follow road to **3. Landrover track climb grid ref. 299059 :** uphill to **4. Junction grid ref 293051 :** turn R to climb up Glen Loin into Coire Grogain and descent to **5. Stream crossing, grid ref 276084 :** Turn R after crossing to short climb & steep loose descent (Deflationator) to climb again and fast descent to **6. Turn off R to bridge, grid ref 303092:** cross bridge R and onto singletrack climb to singletrack descent, onto farm road, keeping L to **7. Signposted path junction, grid ref. 301052 :** Take R branch back to start.

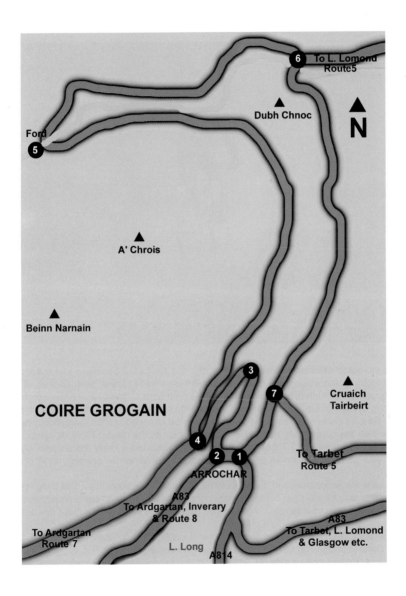

Dubh Chnoc

N

Ford
5

A' Chrois

Beinn Narnain

COIRE GROGAIN

6 To L. Lomond
Route 5

3

7

Cruaich
Tairbeirt

4

2 1

ARROCHAR

To Tarbet
Route 5

A83
To Ardgartan, Inverary
& Route 8

To Ardgartan
Route 7

A83
To Tarbet, L. Lomond
& Glasgow etc.

L. Long

A814

ARDGARTAN
Map OS Landranger Sheet 56
Distance : 38K   Ascent : 1,500m
Skill : Easy / Intermediate   Overall : Challenging
Getting there : from the S A82 then A83, from the N A83

This top-notch excursion takes you right round the Ardgartan peninsula and is based on an early Forestry Commission cycle route. Originally riders had to brave deep ditches, off-camber rooty bits and metre high drop-offs into bottomless peat bogs. These have now been bypassed with a long section of broad singletrack. This provides a year round riding surface. It's still fun though! Despite these alterations, what could never be changed are the magnificent views over Loch Long on the outward leg and those to the Cobbler on the return. The long climbs and fast descents are still there too. Together they combine to provide a really tremendous outing that will test your stamina and nerve on a day where you will either be grunting uphill or grinning downhill.

The wee link we've woven in, to the waterfalls, helps make sure the whole thing is elevated from the ordinary. It's still possible to nip into Lochgoilhead for a bite to eat or a paddle in the sea, if either of these take your fancy. Whatever you decide to do you'll have a great day out!

1. FC car park Glen Croe : Head over the river & uphill to the **2. Junction grid ref. 253041** : turn L & climb to bridge and down to **3. Junction grid ref. 262014** : go R & uphill, following route markers to **4. Coire Lochan grid ref, 218953** : head up broad singletrack with tough climbs and descend to **5. Landrover track grid ref 213979** : Turn R and continue to **6. Junction grid ref. 202014** : Turn R and into forest and waterfalls with short carry before descent to **7. Inveronich Farm** : Turn R & on to B828 to **8. Entry to landrover track, grid ref. 198037** : Turn L and keep climbing to **9. Summit, grid ref 228068** : Head downhill (beware walkers) to **2.** return to start (remember the gate at the bottom).

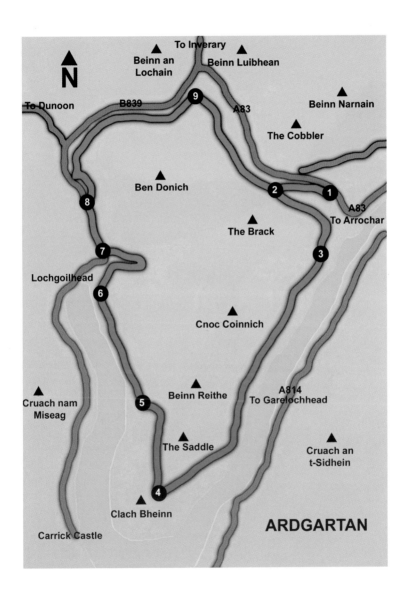

Heading for Corran

Descending to L. Gaineanhach

THE LEACANN MUIR ROAD
Map OS Landranger Sheet 55
Distance : 38K Ascent : 1,100m
Skills : ADVANCED/EXPERT   Overall : Hard
Getting there : From the S A82 (Loch Lomond) then A83 from the N (Oban) A83

The Leacann Muir Road is an all-time classic of Scottish mountain biking and contains every-thing a great route should. As well as fabulous views and excellent riding it has muck and water in abundance. You'll get very dirty at some points. Don't worry the many fords and splashes will soon wash it off. Although you'll get soaked at any time of the year it's not one to be taken lightly in winter as the first dousing arrives early on. Consequently you'll be cold and damp all day. But if that doesn't deter you it should be rideable all year as long as you're prepared to turn back if the crossing of the burn emptying into L.Gaineanhach proves too much.

The actual riding has made or broken quite a few and continues to test anyone who picks up the gauntlet. There's tons of singletrack, it's 100% rideable and offers stiff climbs followed by screaming descents. The big descent of the day has an easier line to the R of the track but for full value the tougher riding down the middle or to the L offers many opportunities to use the full range of handling skills possessed by a competent rider. There's a lull in the action, along the side of Loch Awe, where lunch can be taken before the haul up through the Eredine Forest.

On the final leg, more fabulous singletrack, past yet more lochans, leads to the final (superb) descent which ends close to the start point.

1. Road end opposite Auchndrain Folk Museum, grid ref 029032: Head straight along track to **2. Junction, grid ref 999013:** Trend L and continue on main track to **3. Track end, grid ref. 965005 :** singletrack (wet & wicked) followed by bridge **4. Carron, grid ref. 945997:** Head uphill (tough) onto moorland with stunning loch scenery (photo) followed by steep descent & ford (deep) climb then descend to **5. Junction, grid ref 893031 :** Go R and descend, turning L past Finchairn to **6. B840, grid ref 899041 :** Turn R and head along road to **7. Entry to Eredine Forest, grid ref 962083:** climb, trending R and up to **8. Path to Auchindrain, on R of track, grid ref 986048:** follow singletrack over Eredine summit and out of forest past two lochans and descent to ford with steep climb on opposite side, descend to outward track & turn L .

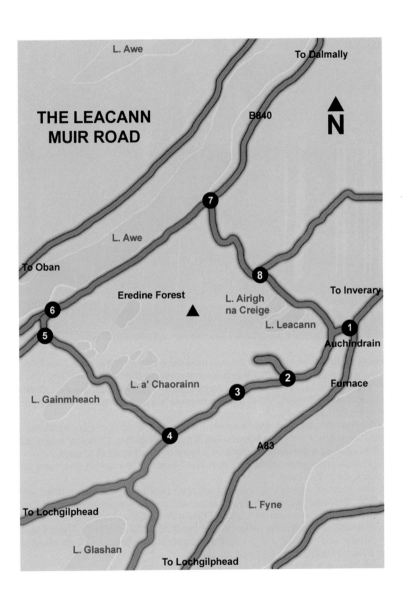

THE LEACANN MUIR ROAD

L. Awe

To Dalmally

B840

N

7

L. Awe

To Oban

8

Eredine Forest

L. Airigh na Creige

To Inverary

L. Leacann

6

1

Auchindrain

5

2

Furnace

L. a' Chaorainn

3

L. Gainmheach

4

A83

To Lochgilphead

L. Fyne

L. Glashan

To Lochgilphead

THE MID-ARGYLL TRAILS
Map OS Landranger Sheet 55
Distance : Various Ascent : Various
Skills : EASY/INTERMEDIATE/ADVANCED/EXPERT   Overall : Your choice
Getting there : From the S A82 (Loch Lomond) then A83. From (Oban) A816 then A83

For many years a large number of marked trails have existed in this area. The forests South of Crinan have been full of family friendly routes that meander from inlet to inlet and onto the open coast with views of the nearby islands. The forests above Lochgilphead, around L.Glashan have several miles of similar terrain.   All of these runs provide lovely riding that is a bit different from the usual forest fire road bash.

In 2005 a new development, the Firetower Trails, was opened above Lochgilphead. Built by the Forestry Commission with help from the Mid Argyll Cycling Club, it's similar in character to the riding centres opened in the borders, albeit on a more compact scale at present.

Through local knowledge, clever use has been made of the terrain and many interesting features add spice to the riding.

You'll find yourself negotiating naturally exposed bedrock or sections pitched with locally sourced stone. Elevated platforms carry you above soft ground in an easy version of Vancouver's 'North Shore' trails. Names such as 'Twisted Firestarter' and 'Swamp Thing' accurately sum up the riding to be experienced none more so than the climb of 'Murder Hill'. There's even a burn to splash through and coupled with the fact that some of the riding is through mixed woodland makes for a less artificial feel to a lot of it.

Although there is a dedicated car park, accessed from the A86 just N of the Cairnbaan junction, the best way to enjoy the trails is to start from the town and approach them from the Dippin Burn. Once you've finished, a pleasant return can be made by heading for Cairnbaan and using the towpath beside the Crinan Canal for a relaxed wind down.

Trail guide leaflets can be picked up at the excellent CrinanCycles, Argyll St, Lochgilphead 01546 603511.

Firetower berms

Ochils climb

10. Carron Valley,
11. Braeval, 12. Glen Finglas,
13. Glen Ample, 14. Choinneachan Hill,
15. Amulree, 16. Glen Devon & the Silver Glen,
17. Glen Garr, 18. Loch Ordie

SOUTHERN AREA MAP

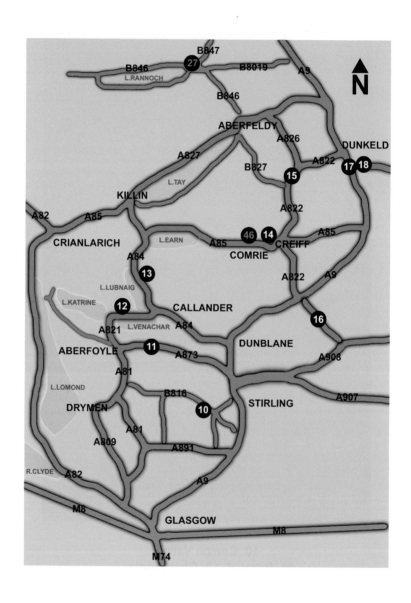

The line of mountains that stretch from the Firth of Clyde to the Firth of Forth marks the boundary between the lush rolling landscape of the Lowlands and the more rugged aspects of the Highlands. The routes within this section lie close to this border and like the majority of outings in the book can be combined with their near neighbours or varied using the alternative tracks shown. All that limits you is your leg strength and imagination.

The section opens near Stirling with the man-made trails at the Carron Valley. Known as the Kelpie Trails they provide a fantastic facility that is easily reached from the central belt and bring dependable, all weather, riding within easy reach of the major population centres. Great views can be enjoyed over to the bulk of the Southern Highlands looming to the North.

The Braeval loop will be familiar to riders who have cut their mountain biking teeth on one of its many variants. The same can be said of its near neighbour, the Glen Finglas loop, which can be added to it or to the Glen Ample circuit to make bigger days. The Finglas trip is a simple traverse of two glens that includes some exceptionally fast downhill sections. The Ample route is a firm favourite with many and one which stands out as a classic.

The Ochils contain much riding and the Glen Devon route takes you into their core to give glimpses of the possibilities. From it you will be able to see Choinneachan Hill, above Crieff, which gives a splendid short day of hard work, lofty views and screaming descents.

Nearby in Amulree a gentler circuit can be enjoyed but that still takes you up a fair old height. It's suitable for those just beginning to feel brave enough to stray from waymarked trails toward the real freedom that a mountain bike can bring.

The two final offerings in this area are centred round the town of Dunkeld. The Glen Garr route contains some of the finest singletrack to be enjoyed anywhere. It has a wide variety of riding which changes from sheltered woodland to exposed moorland trails. A combination that is rare for such a compact circuit. The final route is, strictly speaking, part of the Eastern Highlands. However, it lies so close to the South that its inclusion in the Eastern Highlands section would be incongruous. It's another day that is open to much variation and provides plenty of chances to explore the many alternatives. It's suitable for beginners and experienced riders alike and provides a beautiful excursion into the loch strewn scenery to the North of Dunkeld.

The first of the multi day routes (p 117-127) loops round the centre of the area on mainly easy tracks that bring loads of views and great riding.

CARRON VALLEY

Map OS Landranger Sheet 57
Distance : Various Ascent : Various
Skills : EASY/INTERMEDIATE/ADVANCED/EXPERT   Overall : Your choice
Getting there : From the S M80/A80, follow signs for Kilsyth onto B802 and R on to B818
to join the Tak ma doun Road (signposted) to turn L on to B818 , from N A9/M9 to junct 10
& follow A872 to Denny then the B818

At the time of writing this is the newest addition to the riding centres that are springing up around the country. Set in an area that was once the domain of the hardy riders capable of taking their bikes round Tomtain, Garrel Hill and Meikle Bin, a facility has been created that brings the excitement and fun of mountain biking to a wider audience.

The Carron Valley Development Group has, for the moment, concentrated its efforts in providing some excellent trails above the reservoir in the first phase of a project that will see further extensions added in time. Enticing views to the hills further North can be glimpsed as you make your way around the superb trails that are now in place.

A singletrack approach (above) has been included. Known as "Pipedream" it snakes its way smoothly through the trees easing the effort of the uphill struggle.

The top of the climb lands you at the "Eas Dubh" (Black Waterfall) trail. Apart from one steepish stone-pitched drop there's nothing very technical about it. Even that is just a question of nerve as it has a good run-out at the bottom. Nevertheless, it loops through the trees in countless turns that demand the skill to do them justice. Little dips and drops add more interest to what is one of the most elegant bits of man made trail in the country. It's an absolute joy to ride. "Cannonball Run" is next and is a little faster paced and ends with a big bermed corner spitting you out at the LRT that will carry you to the finale.

"The Fun Park" (opposite) ends the riding in a long series of jumps and bermed (banked) switchbacks. If you take them at full pelt you and your bike will be lofted into the air. However, there's no need to worry if you don't have a pilot's licence, taken more sedately all the features can be negotiated while remaining attached to terra-firma. Fantastic!

Playpark airtime

BRAEVAL LOOP

Map OS Landranger Sheet 57
Distance : 25K   Ascent : 800m
Skill : Easy   **Overall : Challenging**
Getting there : From S A81. From N via A84 (T) then A81 from Callander. Both following
signs for Aberfoyle

Set in the heart of the Trossachs this trip will provide the rider of more modest abilities with a taste of mountain biking away from waymarked trails. Those with more experience may want to try the ST links shown on the map. For this route, an uphill start from the Braeval car park leads to an easy singletrack descent back to the road before the route over to L. Venachar is followed. The Sustran path along its side is gentle, interesting and beautiful. The way back to the start passes close to L. Drunkie where more variation is possible for the inquisitive. Once at the summit, a straightforward blast can be enjoyed back to the start or more singletrack woven into it as taste dictates.

This route can be linked to the Glen Finglas circuit to make a longer day of great quality. It can also be started from the main car park in Aberfoyle. The Braeval start is quieter and allows easy access to the facilities of the town before or after the ride.

1. Braeval car park, grid ref. 541006 : head up LRT from car park and straight ahead to **2. Singletrack entry on R, grid ref 549013 :** Descend singletrack keep going on LRT until A81 is met to turn L and continue to **3. L turn at Portend, grid ref. 571012 :** Head uphill into forest and descent to **4. L turn on to LRT, grid ref. 575042 :** Pass locan on L, through rocky gap to trend R and steep (steep) descent to **5. Gate! , grid ref. 568051 :** Turn L and go along road to enter Sustrans track along Loch Venachar to **6. Junct. Grid ref 537055 :** Turn L and head uphill forest drive to bear L & round gate to follow edge of L. Drunkie to **7. Junct, grid ref, 534046 :** Follow track to **8. R turn, grid ref 538039 :** Keep climbing and go straight through all junctions to return to Braeval.

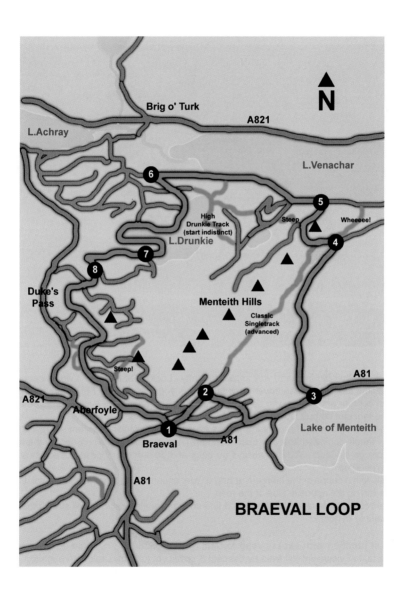

BRAEVAL LOOP

GLEN FINGLAS
Map OS Landranger Sheet 57
Distance : 24K Ascent : 950m
Skills : Easy/Intermediate   Overall : Challenging/Hard
Getting there : From S or E, A821 via Aberfoyle or Callander respectively

This is another old favourite well known to many. Looking at the map it would be all to easy to dismiss the loop as dull landrover track but it's not your usual stuff. For one thing it climbs to the 600m contour and makes you pay the price for it. The reward for such effort is obvious and the speed that can be built up on the way down is truly amazing.

Taken anti-clockwise the climbing is less savage and the initial descent steeper and more exciting. Taken clockwise (the way described here) the climbing is a bit harder but the descending is more continuous. You can always go back and do it in the opposite direction and make your own mind up?

Finish with a cuppa in the tearoom at Brig o' Turk or something more substantial at the excellent Byre Inn on the opposite side of the road.

Linked to the Braeval circuit it makes a fine and challenging day that will stretch the stamina of the majority of riders.

1. A821 at junction with access road to dam, grid ref 536066 : Straight up steep road with welcome rest at viewpoint followed by descent & re-ascent to farm, straight through to
2. Junction with footpath signpost, grid ref. 523104 : Carry straight on (descending) to ford or bridge and then relentless climbing to summit, followed by wild speed

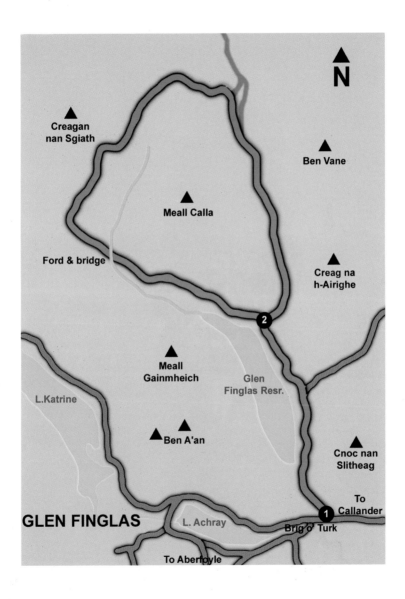

Gleann nam Meannn

Gleann Dubh singletrack

GLEN AMPLE
Map OS Landranger Sheet 57
Distance : 24K Ascent : 950m
Skills : Intermediate/Advanced   **Overall : Challenging/Hard**
Getting there : From N or S A84 via Crialnarich or Callander respectively

In either direction, the traverse of Glen Ample is the classic mountain bike route of the area. For many years it had been a testing ground for budding "hard men" but with the rise in standards and improvement in bikes it no longer holds the same aura in terms of technical difficulty.   What will never change is the quality of the riding and the views to be enjoyed throughout the journey.

Taken anti-clockwise (as described in this route) you'll see the summits of the Ben Lawers group peek above the Loch Earn hills while Stuc a' Chroin towers to your right. The descent of Glen Ample then provides an entertaining set of options for you to explore.

The crossing of the Allt Coire Chroisg nay prove tricky if there has been a lot of rain and another ford lies ahead of that but will be crossable if the 1st one is dispatched. The lower glen is pleasant and the route described takes you to the A84 to pick up a tremendous section of Sustrans route that will sweep you towards Balquhidder where a stop at the tearoom is highly recommended.

The remainder of the route is gentle and scenic and allows you to high and low options along L.Lubnaig. It's a tremendous route that is deservedly popular.

1. Car Park A84 at, grid ref 586107 : Head N on road to take 1st R to **2. Entry to forest on R, grid ref. 587118 :** Carry straight on (ever steeper climbing) through gate onto open hill track and follow it over to Glen Ample passing Glenample farm on the L to **3. Road, grid ref 602225** : Turn L on road to **4. Junction with A84 :** Turn L and follow main road a short dist. to
5. Entry to Sustrans track, grid ref 582221 : Cross A84 & go L onto track to head SW to
6. Road : turn R and head through Balqhuidder, following Sustrans route on road to **7. Strathyre:** Keep on Sustrans track to follow it to bridge back to A84 and L turn to get back to start point.

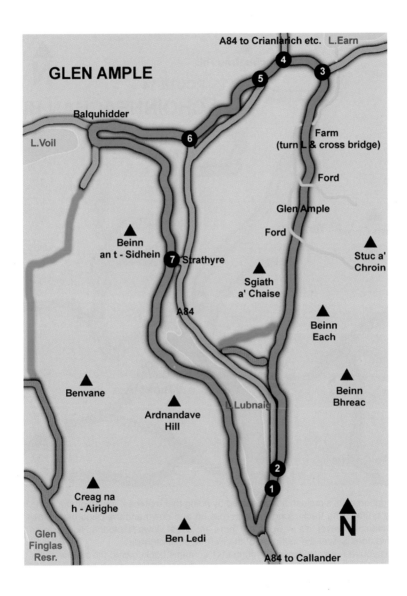

CHOINNECHAN HILL
Map OS Landranger Sheet 52
Distance : 16K   Ascent : 700m
Skill : Easy/Intermediate   Overall : Challenging
Getting there : From S A85 via Loch Earn. From N A9 then A822 via Dunkeld

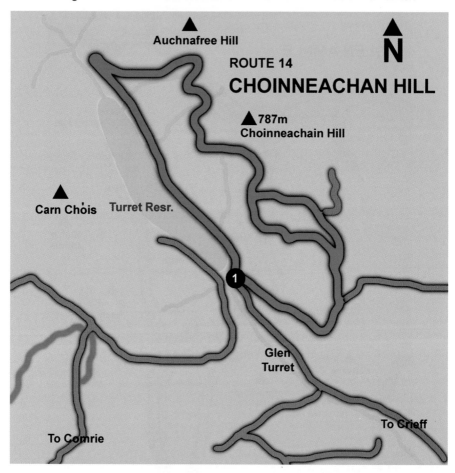

Navigation at its simplest, accompanied by riding that matches. Although the riding is simple it's pretty brutal. The track along the loch rolls up and down and the climb that follows will test your stamina. However, it's all worth it. There are Great views N into the Highlands and equally impressive ones S over the lushness of the Perthsire countryside.

When you're ready to descend, rough LRT screams back toward the start with the option of taking the L branch half way down. However, straight ahead is probably best for those who don't like incinerating their brake pads. Keep trending R to take you back to the car park.

1. Turret Dam car park, grid ref 821265 : Leave car park, head for side of reservoir, ride along E side of reservoir, take only turn on R, climb big hill, ride down big hill. Whahey!

AMULREE

Map OS Landranger Sheet 52
Distance : 25K Ascent : 720m
Skills : Easy   Overall : Moderate/Challenging
Getting there : From S A822 via Crieff, E A822 via Dunkeld, N A826 via Aberfeldy

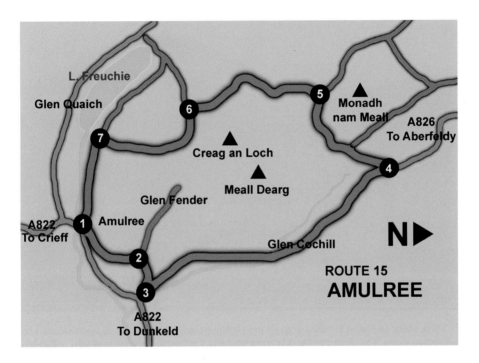

For anyone looking for an introduction to high open ground, with spectacular views, this might do the job. The navigation is straightforward, especially if the road is taken from Amulree for a direct entry to Glen Cochill. However, it would be a pity to miss the initial part which is good fun.

Glen Cochill allows the bulk of the height to be gained on a smooth and relatively quiet road before heading through the forest back over the hills to Glen Quaich.

As you leave the forest you'll see Loch Hoil and Schiehallion in the distance behind it. From there a relatively short haul up to the route's high point allows views over Glen Quaich to the craggy defile of Glen Lochan. A speedy drop takes you to Glen Quaich and the run home.

1. Parking near Hotel, Amulree : Roll downhill from the hotel, cross bridge and enter track system between farm buildings on L, keep ploughing straight ahead over rough ground and bumpy descent to bridge over Glenfender Burn to climb (stile) to **2. LRT grid ref. 908384:** R turn onto landrover track which is followed to **3. Junct. with A826 at Milton, grid ref. 917386 :** Turn L up Glen Cochill and turn L near its head to **3. Entry to forest, grid ref. 886451 :** squeeze through gate and head straight uphill to **5. Gate & junct. grid ref. 866433 :** Turn L and head for high pass and fine views into glen Quaich, descend (fast) over wooden bridge to **6. Junction, grid ref, 870397 :** turn L for one last climb and descent (beware2 gates) to **7. Junction, grid ref 880372 :** Turn L and head back to start.

GLEN DEVON AND THE SILVER GLEN
Map OS Landranger Sheet 57
Distance : 35K Ascent : 1,250m
Skills : Intermediate/Advanced Overall : Hard
Getting there : From N or S, A9 via Gleneagles, or train to Gleneagles Stn.

This route stands at the very edge of the Highlands and is dominated by open slopes and expansive views. The climb from Alva is a monster and it is best to have the legs warmed up before attempting it. This is the main reason for beginning the day from the N which also provides straightforward access from the A9 corridor.

The ascent, up the front face of the Ochils is brutal. Once the first section of it is complete you are transported to the open spaces of Glen Winnel (above). More hard work follows getting onto the summits of Ben Buck and Ben Cleuch before the series of descents leading back to the start.

The day demands dry conditions of hard frost or drought. Parts of it are popular with walkers but the descents are open and anyone else using the paths is easily seen.

Starting from Gleneagles station adds 13K and 150m climbing to the day.

1. A823 at track end, grid ref 949053 : Head along road to **2. Exit to track near Borland, grid ref. 984048 :** Exit R and struggle up above Burnfoot to enter Glen Quey and descent to Dollar to pick up cycle track leading to Tillicoultry to **3. Junction with A908, grid ref. 921967 :** turn R & up to A91 & left to track running up R (E) side of golf course to **4. Junction, grid ref. 897975 :** Steep climbing now up well surfaced track to break out from trees and onto open hillside with murderous zig zags to continue to **5. Bend in track and exit E onto hillside, grid ref 889010 :** Head E onto open hillside and climb as best you can up path (soft if damp) to Ben Buck and on to the summit of Ben Cleuch followed by descent to **6. Watershed between Skythorn & Andrew Gannel Hills, grid ref 923010 :** Descend N and follow landrover track at bottom E to start point.

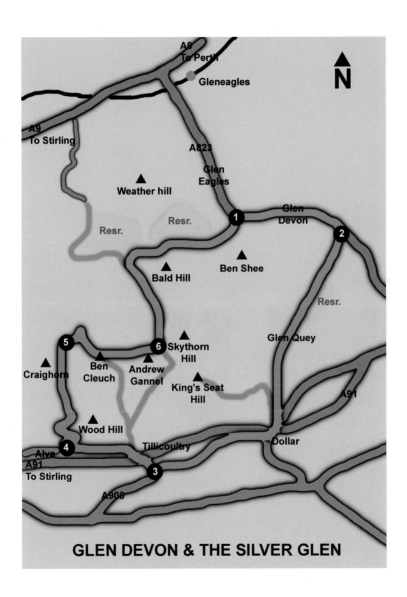

GLEN DEVON & THE SILVER GLEN

Nearing Ben Cleuch summit

Ochil Descent

GLEN GARR
Map OS Landranger Sheet 52
Distance : 25K Ascent : 650m
Skills : Intermediate/Advanced   Overall : Challenging
Getting there : From S or N, A9 84 or train to Dunkeld Station

Any circuit that includes the descent of Glen Garr is always going to be a cracker. Starting at Dunkeld railway station, this particular version takes you through Birnam Wood and on to the Hermitage which sits above the river Braan. The route described avoids the busiest lower section of that tourist trap and takes you up to the spectacular Rumbling Bridge with plenty of interest along the way. After this you head for the ancient path that will see you cross the watershed to Glen Garr. Superb riding follows (shown above & frontispiece) and a stop can be enjoyed in Bankfoot before the homeward leg.

The last section takes you into Birnam Wood once more for some fabulous woodland single-track riding. It's one of the best!

1. Dunkeld Station : Head out of the car park and turn L up the track system along the Inchewan Burn a signposted system takes you over the burn to **2. Car park off minor road below A822, grid ref. 015419 :** Exit car park at far end and onto ST system that leads over the Braan to head uphill and over Rumbling Bridge & 1st L onto ST to take 1st R to **3. A822Road , grid ref 999417 :** Cross road & onto LRT to follow signs past Balhomish to Glen Garr and ST descent to LRT & on to **4. Bankfoot Village & B867 :** Exit village on track leading to Gelly and back to B867 at Bee Cottage and entry to **5. LRT on W side of B867, grid ref 053391 :** Enter track system which leads to **6. Path on R, grid ref. 042399:** Signposted return with much ST.

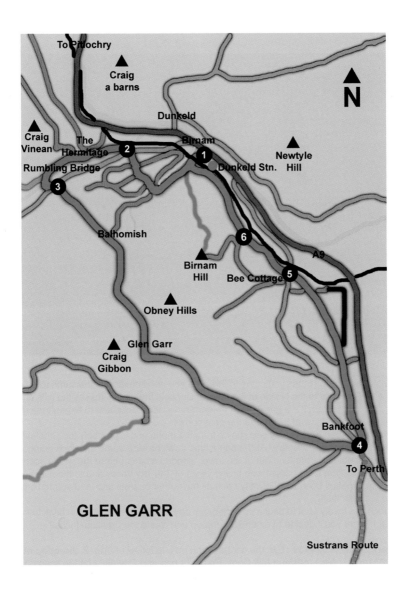

GLEN GARR

LOCH ORDIE
Map OS Landranger Sheet 52
Distance : 19K   Ascent : 470m
Skill : Easy   Overall : Moderate
Getting there : From S or N, A9 to Dunkeld then follow A923 (Blairgowrie) and follow signs to car park

No mater how many times you come to this area you need never ride the same route twice. A complex of LRTs exists to the N side of the town of Dunkeld that criss-crosses the hills and moors above it. For this reason it's a great place to learn navigation skills and to experience the joy of finding out, for yourself, what lies round the next corner.

The trip described here is only one choice from the menu and is probably the simplest that will show you the best of the scenery. At the same time it will provide some excellent riding.

The route begins by climbing out of the lower wooded slopes before the whole scene opens up. Once it does, you find yourself with broad views of the Tay Valley and to the hills beyond.

Mill Dam, Rotmell Loch and Dowally Loch all have their charms and lead you to Raor Lodge and on to L. Ordie itself.

The loch is a lovely spot to pause on a pleasant day before enjoying the run back to the valley below. Or maybe you'll decide to extend the trip up and round the Ossinian lochs?

1. Car Park, grid ref 024439 : Exit the car park and go L to follow LRT to **2. Junction at Glaick, grid ref 031462 :** Go L passing Mill Dam, Rotmell Loch and Dowally Loch to reach **3. Junct. Below Raor Lodge, grid ref, 016479 :** Go R and trend L as you meet L. Ordie to **4. Turn off R along N shore of loch, grid ref. 031505 :** Go round loch to **5. Lochordie Lodge, grid ref 030497 :** Turn L and head back past Mill Dam to **2.** And retrace 1st leg back to car park.

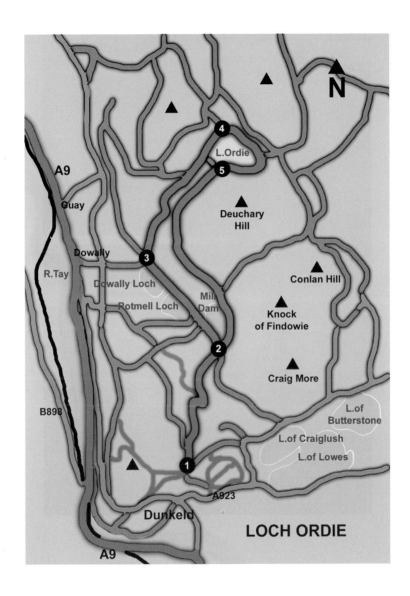

The head of L. Pattack

**19. Glen Kinglass & Glen Orchy,
20. The Devil's Staircase, 21. The Ciaran Path,
22. The Leanacahan Forest, 23. Loch Ossian, 24. Glen Bogle,
25. Laggan Wolf Trax, 26. Ben Alder,
27. Loch Garry**

CENTRAL HIGHLANDS AREA MAP

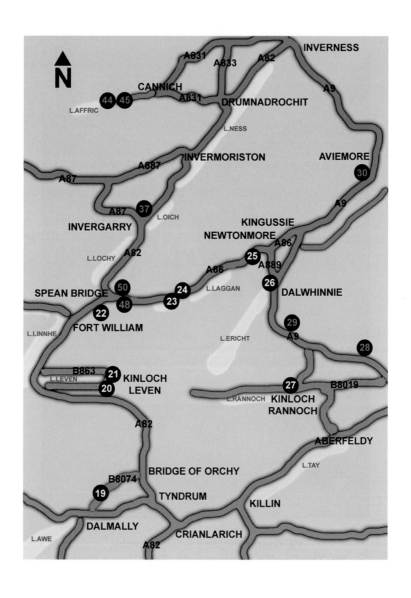

The Central Highlands contain many of the hills and cliffs most prized by walkers and mountaineers. The The Blackmount, the Mamores, The Aonachs, Ben Nevis and Glen Coe all lie within their bounds. The area is also dominated by Rannoch moor; one of the biggest areas of wild land in the UK. The result is that the amount of available mountain biking is perhaps a little less than that which might have been anticipated. No worries though, the trails that do exist contain riding and scenery that are the match of anything elsewhere and have choices for all grades of rider.

The Glen Kinglass circuit is a superb day for the fit. It shows off Loch Etive and the Blackmount hills with tons of riding interest thrown in. The Devil's Staircase is a route that every mountain biker should do. It travels the length of Glencoe and finishes with some really exciting descending. The Ciaran Path, the tail end of which can be tacked on to "The Staircase", is a magical experience if you're up for it.

Round past Fort William the trails in the Leanachan Forest offer everything from family friendly riding to the full-on thrill of the World cup downhill course and a ski lift to transport you to its top. This is contrasted by the gentle trip out to Loch Ossian; with no technical difficulties it's still a fabulous route. Starting from the same point the "Glen Bogle" circuit is a true high mountain route that will stretch many. The Laggan Wolf Trax, at the far end of Glen Spean, is another stunning man made facility that offers plenty for all.

Moving round to Dalwhinnie the circuit of Ben Alder is a day to be taken seriously but will bring rich reward to those who tackle it and venture round one of Scotland's most remote mountains.

The final offering is a route passing by Loch Garry. Although the bulk of the riding is pretty easy it passes through some stunning landscapes. The spectacular views are coupled to some great big fast and hairy descents.

The multi day routes which pass through the area amplify all of the above. The Loch Etive trip travels the length of that loch and then tackles Glen Kinglass in the opposite direction to the one day route. The Luibeilt Loop provides some of the most fantastic singletrack and scenery for those strong enough to contemplate it.

GLEN KINGLASS
Map OS Landranger Sheet 50
Distance : 80K   Ascent : 1,700m
Skill : Intermediate   Overall : Epic
Getting there : From S A82 to Tyndrum then A85 to take B8074. From N, A82 to B8074 1K
S of Bridge of Orchy

Experienced hands will be familiar with the concept of epics. Some arise from misfortune but those that are deliberately sought out must present obvious challenges for the rider to test their mettle. They must also have one or more elements that make all the work worthwhile. This is one such route and the first full-blooded epic to be included in the book.

However you look at it 80k is an epic undertaking in a single day. For the effort expended you'll be rewarded with stunning views and excellent riding. Even the long road section at the start manages to be a bit special. The ensuing track along Loch Etive will leave you gasping in wonder at the scenery.

Glen Kinglas is a joy that contains some lovely riding. The mountain scene around Loch Dochart is amazing and will breathe life back into the tiredest rider.

Most of the journey is on relatively smooth surfaces but between Glenkinglass Lodge and the short section of LRT to Victoria bridge the way forward requires some skill and thought.

For those in need of resuscitation the Iveroran and Bridge of Orchy Hotels provide refuge and sustenance before the final leg down Glen Orchy. This is far more interesting and demanding than you might at first think. It involves the crossing of several streams and a speedy blast back to the start point bringing a superb day to an exciting conclusion!

1. B8704, Eas Urchaidh car park, grid ref 243320 : CR out of car park & along road to join A85 at **2. Junction, grid ref 197276** : R turn, take care busy road, follow to **3. Signpost for Inverawe, grid ref 031299** : Follow road to **4. R turn into forest, grid ref 025317** : along undulating track to **5. Bridge over R. Kinglass, grid ref 079375** : Turn R and head up glen to **6. Bridge over Abhainn Shira, grid ref 232418** : cross bridge and go R through Victoria Br. And Inveroran and on to **7. Bridge of Orchy, grid ref, 296397** : Don't cross bridge, go through obvious gate and follow signs for cycle route back to the start.

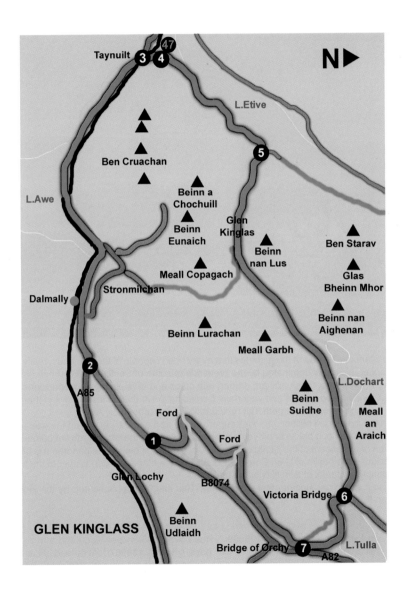

N▶

Taynuilt **3** **4** **47**

L.Etive

5

Ben Cruachan

L.Awe

Beinn a
Chochuill

Glen
Kinglas

Beinn
Eunaich

Beinn
nan Lus

Ben Starav

Meall Copagach

Stronmilchan

Glas
Bheinn Mhor

Dalmally

Beinn nan
Aighenan

Beinn Lurachan

Meall Garbh

L.Dochart

2

A85

Beinn
Suidhe

Meall
an
Araich

Ford

1

Ford

Glen Lochy

B8074

Victoria Bridge **6**

GLEN KINGLASS

Beinn
Udlaidh

Bridge of Orchy **7**

L.Tulla

A82

THE DEVIL'S STAIRCASE
OS Landranger Sheet 41
Distance : 33K   Ascent : 1,200m
Skills : Advanced   Overall : Hard
Getting there : From S or N A82 then B863 from Ballachuillish

"The Staircase" is one of those routes that every rider, capable of the demands, really must do at least once. It's a day dominated by the presence of some of Scotland's finest mountains and, especially in Glen Coe, those hills are draped with crags and cliffs. In the right conditions they will have mist swirling about them and waterfalls cascading down their sides. Views of them can be enjoyed from the safety of the path that runs parallel to the often busy A82.

Even the initial road section provides superb vistas as it carries you toward the main event. It allows views to the loch below and over to Ardgour. However, the biggest reward comes with the completion of the ascent of the Staircase itself. Once this is achieved the panorama is breathtaking. It includes the peaks of Glen Coe, the Buchaille Etive Mor and extends over to the Mamores to the omnipresent bulk of Ben Nevis and beyond.

To cap it all an astounding descent follows. This can be supplemented by the inclusion of the Ciaran Path.

1. Kinlochleven : Loads of places to park, head W along the B836 on the S side of L. Leven to **2. Entry to track on L, grid ref. 105599 :** Head over to Glencoe village and turn L, heading past the Clachaig Hotel & cross A82 to **3. Car park, grid ref. 138567 :** At far end of car park join path on N side of road and follow it up the glen, exiting at highest car park and onto A82 for short distance to **4. Exit on L onto old road, grid ref 179565 :** Climb to study (fine viewpoint) and along old road to join A82 once more and follow this to **5. Foot of the Devils' Staircase, grid ref 220563 :** Ride up as much as you can to pause at the summit & gawp at the views before following your front wheel all the way down. May be busy with walkers.

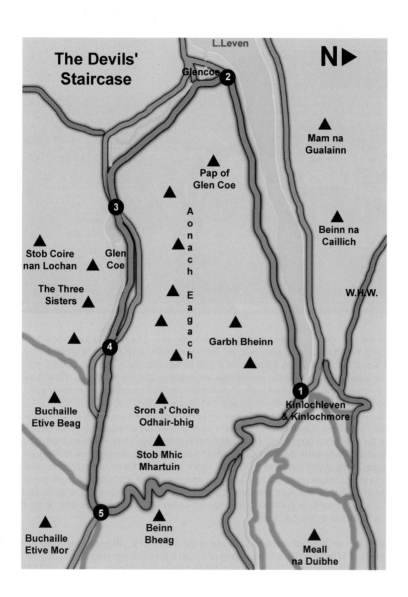

THE CIARAN PATH
Map OS Landranger Sheet 41
Distance : 40K   Ascent : 1,100m
Skill : Expert +   Overall : Hard
Getting there : From S or N, A82 then B863 to Kinlochleven/Kinlochmore

There are not enough superlatives to describe this day. The riding is fantastic and scenically there is next to nothing to compare with it. The view down Loch Leven is breathtaking and the easy roll along the sides of the Eilde lochs is just as spectacular. Then, at Luibeilt you begin to feel the isolation as you cross the sometimes impossible Abhainn Rath (pic) where you are sur-rounded by more peaks. The faint path on its N side can be frustrating in the upper part but gives some good riding in the lower section or you can cross at Staoineag bothy.

At the loch, a bridge leads to LRT and on to the singletrack path which will take you to the Blackwater Reservoir. It's superb and there's even shelter to be had in the bothy near the reser-voir while the Glen Coe peaks occupy the horizon in a way you've never seen them before.

Once at the Blackwater dam the Ciaran Path lies below. It's certainly not for the faint hearted and contains some pretty demanding riding. There are some fierce rock and drainage features to be negotiated. Some nasty off camber rock, steep sections and slippery roots mean that dry conditions are best. In the right conditions, for the skilful, it's a stunning climax to an astound-ing day! If courage fails, or common sense dictates, the LRT above the S side of the R. Leven provides a fast route to the day's end.

1. Kinlochleven or Kinlochmore : Head round the B836 to **2. Signposted road to Mamore Lodge, grid ref 176623 :** Climb to the lodge and past it & onto the crest before Loch Eilde Mor to follow LRT to **3. Ford near Luibeilt (impassible in heavy conditions), grid ref. 263685 :** Cross Abhainn Rath and down demanding singletrack to cross bridge at bottom onto LRT and head for **4. Junction with path to BlackwaterDam, grid ref 320687 :** Follow path with excellent riding and stunning Glen Coe Views to **6. Blackwater Dam :** Descend Ciaran Path (expert riders only) and follow it, above the N side of the River Leven, into town.

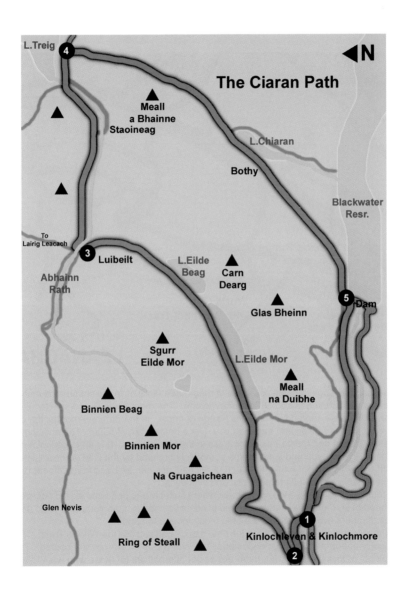

The Ciaran Path

LEANACHAN FOREST
Map OS Landranger Sheets 41
Distance : Variable   Ascent : Variable
Skill : Easy/Intermediate/Advanced/Expert   Overall : Your Choice
Getting there : From S or N (West) A82, from East A9 to Dalwhinnie or Kingussie
followed by A86

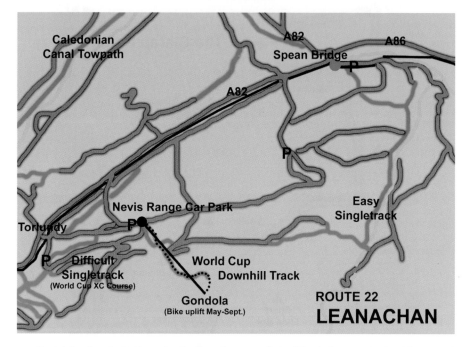

Containing the single biggest collection of man-made facilities in the country the riding based in the Leanachan forest has something for everyone. The most obvious and spectacular facility is the downhill course served by the Nevis Range gondola. In the Summer months the capsules are converted to carry bikes and transport you over a height gain of 550m. The ensuing descent is one of the fastest and most demanding trails in the whole world. It is an experience not to be missed and will leave you and your brakes completely pumped by the time you complete it. For those with the skills but not a bike to match, a full package can be hired from Offbeat Bikes that includes a suitable steed, full protective kit and a lift pass.

The four cross (4 X) is a short, wide, track where suitably equipped and skilled riders can race head to head over, round and above a series of obstacles and is a fabulous spot to go and watch the antics of others even if it proves a bit too much for you to handle.

For the less gravity inspired rider, a fun time can be had tackling the Witch's Trails. These are cross-country oriented routes that encompass the World Cup cross- country course. They still contain plenty of tricky sections but there are easier alternatives for those who want to avoid the hardest parts. These are all supplemented by a huge complex of easier riding within the forest itself that includes loads of straightforward singletrack and even a Trailquest (bike orienteering) course.

Throw in free parking, civilised facilities including a 1st rate café, and you have an amazing place to visit and ride.

Map OS Landranger Sheets 41 & 42
Distance : 49K   Ascent : 550m
Skill : Easy   Overall : Challenging/Hard
Getting there : From W A82 to Fort William then A86 to Moy. From E A9 to Newtonmore
then A86 as above

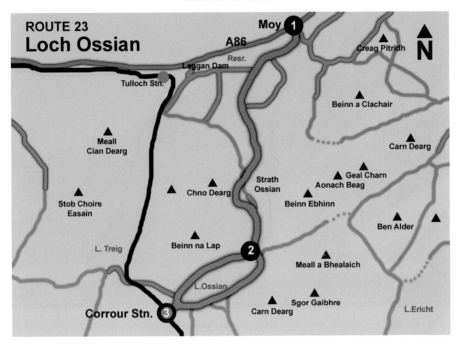

For riders of modest abilities this route provides a chance to penetrate deep into the mountains without the worry of technical difficulties. The whole journey is on well surfaced LRT and easy to follow.

Strath Ossian itself is a wild and beautiful place but when the loch is reached you will learn why the area is held in such high regard by hill walkers and all who love mountain scenery.

The view down L.Ossian from the youth hostel is, without doubt, one of the classics. It is a place to linger and absorb your surroundings before setting off back home. The hostel is also one of the loveliest around and a great favourite with any who have been lucky enough to stay there.

Until relatively recently Corrour station had a restaurant on the platform. The estate closed this and the bunkouse removing two fabulous facilities. The estate has a number of up-market cottages for rent for those who want to stay in the area. The platform is worth a visit as a viewpoint and for fans of the film Trainspotting in which it appeared.

For the time being, and for those with less deep pockets, the SYHA hostel remains a magical place to spend a night.

1. Moy Car Park, grid ref 433831 : Follow LRT past Luiblea and into forest, keeping dead ahead until you reach **2. Junction at E end of L.Ossian, grid ref 411698 :** Make decision of clockwise or anti-clockwise circuit of loch and head for **3. Corrour Stn, gird ref 365664 :** reverse outward route using the side of the loch not taken on outward journey.

GLEN BOGLE
Map OS Landranger Sheet 42
Distance : 50K   Ascent : 1,200m
Skills : EXPERT Overall : Hard/Epic
Getting there : from the W A82 then A86, from the E A9 then A86 from Dalwhinnie

In the right conditions, and for those strong and skilled enough, this route will provide one of the best days of mountain biking you could ever hope to enjoy. The name is derived from the fact that it tracks through the mountains where the fictitious Glen Bogle (of the BBC series Monarch of the Glen) lies.

On a clear day its scenery will have you speechless and with firm trails the riding is superb.

The approach, through the area surrounding Loch na-h-Earba, along the River Pattack and into the open ground round the loch of the same name is as varied as it is spectacular. There are several alternatives that can be seen on the map opposite but they way described allows for the best of the scenery to be taken in as well as a visit to the golden sands of the beach at the E end of Loch Laggan. The final descents polish it all off neatly with a bit of adrenaline,

It's a high mountain route, with all the extra considerations this entails. In the dry conditions that are essential (to avoid damage to soft sections) no river crossing will pose a problem.

1. Moy A84, grid ref 432831 : From the parking area head up the track to Lochan-h-Earba & descend to **2. Junction, grid ref. 509874** : Go R & avoid Ardverikie House & make your way to **3. Junction grid ref 553894** : Climb beside the river Pattack and past the Loch of the same name & on to **4. Junction grid ref 545789** : Descend to ford river (or cross by bridge), follow loch margin to **5. Junction , grid ref 520788** : Turn r and head up to descent to a fording of the Allt Cam and a brief carry before riding to **6. Descent to ford, grid ref 511792** : climb out of the gully and ride to the Bealach Leamhainn and a descent to **7. Track junction, grid ref 489800** : Climb path to descend Moy Corrie & an exit L onto the outward route.

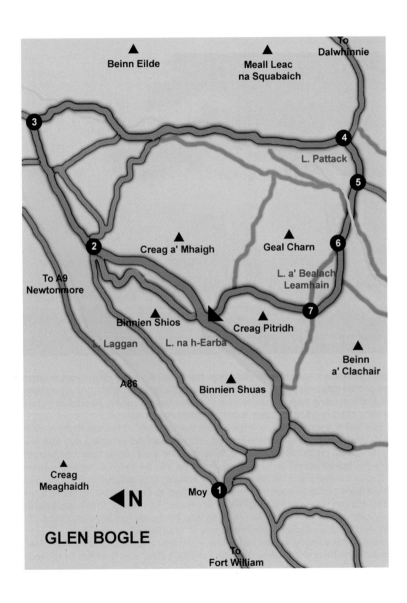

Beinn Eilde

Meall Leac
na Squabaich

To
Dalwhinnie

3

4

L. Pattack

5

Creag a' Mhaigh

Geal Charn

6

L. a' Bealach
Leamhain

2

To A9
Newtonmore

7

Binnien Shios

Creag Pitridh

L. Laggan

L. na h-Earba

Beinn
a' Clachair

A86

Binnien Shuas

Creag
Meaghaidh

◄N

Moy

1

GLEN BOGLE

To
Fort William

LAGGAN WOLFTRAX
Map OS Landranger Sheet 42
Distance : Variable Ascent : Variable
Skill : Intermediate/ Advanced/ Expert   Overall : Your choice
Getting there : A9 (S) off at Dalwhinnie then A889 followed by A86, from N off at Kingussie onto A86.   From West Coast A82 to pick up A86 at Spean Bridge

Situated in Strathmashie near Newtonmore this purpose- built riding venue is smack dab in the middle of the Highlands and surrounded by loads of wilderness trails. Anyone planning a trip to sample Scottish riding could do worse than base themselves near it. At present there are three separate trails offering riding for every standard of mountain biker.

The Blue trail is a wide, rolling and open track that is designed to allow those of modest abilities to enjoy it with both wheels on the ground. It's also laid out in such a way that speedsters can hammer it to get plenty of air-time. The table tops and gaps can be launched over rather than rolled through. Speed carried through, to stuff the bike into the bermed (banked) corners.

The Red is narrower and contains plenty of features that require good handling skills. Although it contains plenty of rock features it's designed to flow and be ridden at a reasonable speed. There is one black graded feature on it known as "Air's Rock." This is great big scary slab of naturally outcropping rock which can be bypassed if it proves just too intimidating. The whole thing finishes off with a couple of hundred metres of "boardwalk."

The black trail is a testing ground for the brave and the competent. With features like "Stiletto" (pic opposite) "The Devil's Chessboard" , "The Surgeon's Slab" and "Two Ton Drop" you know it's going to be a bit of a challenge.   There are no chicken runs to the sides of these features which will stretch you and your bike to their limits.

All of this is free and accessible to everyone. When you add in the fact that there is a café, a bike shop (in the shape of Basecamp MTB) and a weekend shuttle service to take you to the top (fee) it's one to add to your list.

Stilletto

BEN ALDER
Map OS Landranger Sheet 42
Distance : 53K   Ascent : 1,450m
Skill : Advanced   Overall : Epic
Getting there : From S or N A9 to Dalwhinnie

There are routes that can only be ridden on a mountain bike and those which can only be ridden by true mountain bikers. This trip falls into the latter category. With a high point of nearly 900m and a carry in the middle of 2k with a 400m height gain it's not everyone's cup of tea but for those with the 'right stuff' it's a fabulous expedition.

The riding is straightforward up to Culra Bothy. After this famous mountaineer's shelter the way ahead becomes more demanding. Pedalling becomes impossible at a severe steeping but it's just a short carry to the top. You are now at the Bealach Dubh and an exciting descent lies on the other side. If your bunny-hopping technique is found wanting you'll be fixing punctures or nursing a wrecked wheel. A lovely ascent to the next bealach follows and leads to a fabulous descent toward L. Ericht.

Unless you intend to visit Ben Alder Cottage a turn off L is made for the punishment of lugging the bike up to the Bealach Breabag to the descent on its far side. You will be rewarded with magnificent views of Ben Alder's North face and some superb riding to follow.

It's a serious route that requires sound mountain sense as well as strength, fitness and handling skills.

1. Dalwhinnie : Cross the railway at the level crossing and head out past Ben Alder Loge to
2. Junct. above L. Patack, grid ref 549787 : turn L & descend to ford river if it is low or use bridge, splash along loch margins to pick up track to Culra bothy where ST begins and steepens below **3. The Bealach Dubh, grid ref 481733 :** Descend (many water bars) then re-ascend to Bealach Cumhann & descend to **4. Path to Bealach Breabag, grid ref. 498681 :** Shoulder bike & walk to bealach, descend to lochan below (initially trackless: walk first section if soft) steep descending after loch leads to **5. Path junct. with option to cross to Culra, grid ref. 562763 :** Either over to Culra and outward track or straight on to LRT to Dalwhinnie.

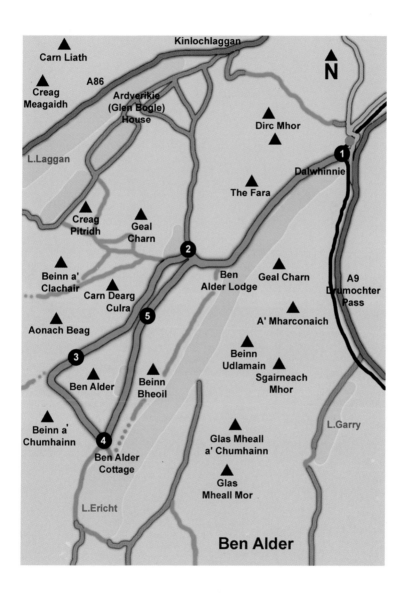

Bealach Breabag descent

LOCH GARRY

Map OS Landranger Sheet 42

Distance : 48K   Ascent : 980m

Skill : Easy   Overall : Hard

Getting there : From S or N A9 to Pitlochry then B8019 to Tummel Bridge followed by B846 to start point

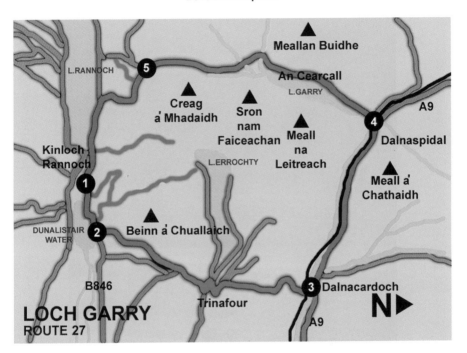

The approach to this route, via the B8019 is one of the loveliest drives in the whole country. It twists and turns through beautiful woodlands and presents amazing views of the lochs it passes. Once Kinloch Rannoch is reached it is worthwhile to make a diversion to the E end of Loch Rannoch for the superb vista it commands.

The first section of the outward leg is hard work on tarmac but it's usually quiet and has a superb road descent down to Trinafour to reward the effort. Once you reach Dalnacardoch the character of the route begins to change. Dalnaspidal is reached using the Sustrans track and from there the day's main feature can be seen. The length of Loch Garry stretches into the distance and the way ahead lies on its West bank. Straightforward riding through magnificent scenery leads to the eye-watering drop back to Loch Rannoch. Don't worry if you get too excited, and miss the last waypoint, you'll end up on the road anyway.

1. Car park, East of Kinloch Rannoch, grid ref 668588 : Head E along B846 to **2. Junct. With B847, grid ref 699589 :** Turn l and head uphill with big descent to Trinafour and on to **3. Dalnacardoch, grid ref 723703 :** Turn L up Sustrans path beside A9 to **4. Dalnaspidal, grid ref 646733 :** Break L from Sustrans path towards L. Garry, along LRT to descent toward L. Rannoch to **5. LRT Junct. grid ref. 620618 :** Take L fork and descend to road & L turn back to start.

Glen Clova

**28. Glen Tilt, 29. The Gaick Pass,
30. The Burma Road, 31. Loch an Eielin,
32. Loch Einich, 33. Glen More,
34. Inshriach, 35. The Fungle,
36. Loch Muick**

EASTERN HIGHLANDS AREA MAP

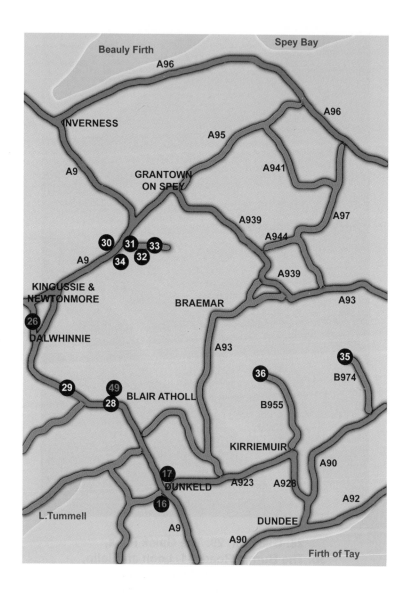

The Eastern Highlands encompasses an enormous area that has two distinct approaches. The approach from the A9 is most convenient for the purpose of this book as it also allows access to the Southern, Central and Northern hills. The final two routes require the eastern approach from the A90 to be used.

Starting in Blair Atholl the Glen Tilt excursion is one of the best and provides just about everything you'd want in a big mountain bike route. Moving up the A9, its near neighbour, the Gaick and Feshie loop takes an epic tour through some magnificent scenery on a route that is mainly comprised of easy riding. For many, the singletrack beside Loch An Dun will be one of the highlights but can easily be walked by those not quite up to the demands.

From there we move up to near Aviemore and kick off with the Burma Road. It's been a favourite with riders for many years and one which ends with an brake cooking descent. It contrasts sharply with the gentle riding round Loch an Eilein just across the road. That wee route still provides plenty of options for those looking for sterner stuff and has some challenges waiting for anyone wanting to explore. It can be linked to the Loch Einich trip which is a simple out and back into some glorious scenery.

Nearby, the Glen More circuit pops in and out of the tree cover with glimpses of the Cairngorm massif accompanying some superb singletrack action. The final route, near Aviemore, is the a round of the Inshriach Forest. It represents all that is best in the sheltered riding available in the vicinity. The singletrack descents are among the best in the country and plenty more are there for those who want to look.

The last two routes move over to the other side of the Eastern hills to tackle stupendous circuits that will be the equal of any in your experience. The Loch Muick route gives one of the finest days of riding in the land and will test your skill. The long day needed for the Fungle and Mounth trip is an epic undertaking that will need all your strength to conquer.

The two day trip, traversing Gaick, Feshie, Geldie and Tilt is one of the best two day routes anywhere. It will test stamina and handling abilities in equal measures.

GLEN TILT
Map OS Landranger Sheet 43
Distance : 54K   Ascent : 1,600m
Skill : Advanced   **Overall : Hard/Epic**
Getting there : From S or N A9 to Blair Atholl, signs for bridge of Tilt car park

The circuit of Glen Tilt is one of the Greats of Scottish mountain biking. It can be tackled in either direction but it's best to go anti-clockwise. Descents seem more continuous and the singletrack from Fealar lodge to the crossing of the Allt Garbh Buidhe is superb in the dry conditions that the day should be reserved for. The estate asks that when the going is soft that bikes be carries on this particular stretch. A precaution most thoughtful riders would adopt in any case. An additional reason for looking for dry conditions is that the river crossing may be difficult or impossible when the water is high.

The initial haul up the road to Loch Moraig is brutal. From there on it's 100% off road action for the rest of way.

To describe the remainder of the route adequately would take up pages and pages. There is a huge variety of trail surface with loads of singletrack and twintrack to add interest.

It should be enough to say that you'll be working hard all day and enjoy fantastic riding in superb surroundings on a route everybody comes back to time and time again.

1. Bridge of tilt car park, grid ref 875663 : R out of the car park over Br. 1st L then uphill past L.Moraig to **2. Gate on R , grid ref 907672 :** Follow LRT to **3. Junct, grid ref 940683 :** Turn R & descend then up to **4. L turn onto rough vehicle track, grid ref 952673 :** Follow track all the way to **5. Daldhu, grid ref. 026704 :** Descend to follow singletrack along loch, down Gleann Mor to **6. Fealar Lodge, grid ref 009799 :** Skirt below farm to pick up singletrack (walk this if it's soft) heading L (SW) below it, on to crossing of Allt Garbh Buidhe (sometimes dangerous) and down Glen Tilt to **7. Bridge, grid ref 881685 :** follow LRT to start point.

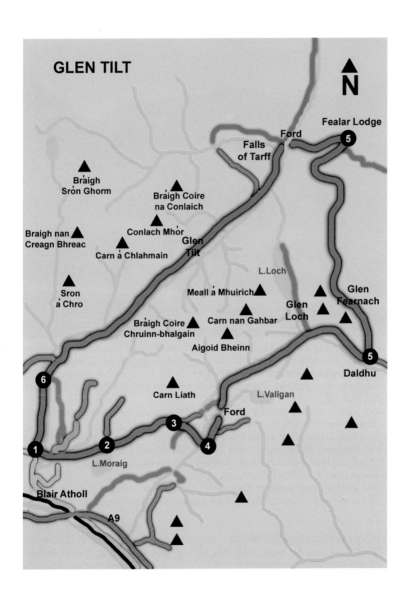

GLEN TILT

N

Fealar Lodge
5

Ford
Falls
of Tarff

Bràigh
Sròn Ghorm

Bràigh Coire
na Conlaich

Braigh nan
Creagn Bhreac

Conlach Mhòr

Carn à Chlahmain

Glen
Tilt

L.Loch

Sron
à Chro

Meall à Mhuirich

Glen
Fearnach

Glen
Loch

Bràigh Coire
Chruinn-bhalgain

Carn nan Gahbar

5

Aigoid Bheinn

Daldhu

6

Carn Liath

L.Valigan

Ford

3

4

5

1

2

L.Moraig

Blair Atholl

A9

THE GAICK PASS
Map OS Landranger Sheets 35 & 42
Distance : 80K   Ascent : 1,200m
Skill : Intermediate/ Advanced   Overall : Epic
Getting there : From S or N, A9 to Dalanasipdal

The Gaick pass is one of the Highlands' most spectacular and historic through routes. Combined with the largely traffic free Sustrans route between Kingussie and Dalnacardoch, it makes an outstanding expedition where fitness and resilience are more important than technical ability. Navigation is pretty straightforward and the whole provides an ideal opportunity to test yourself on a real epic ride.

The start point is chosen to allow pit stops for the weary in Kingussie, Newtonmore or Dalwhinnie at times when they are most likely to be needed.

Setting off from Dalnaspidal allows the legs to warm up briefly before the ascent to the awesome cleft of the Gaick Pass itself. Once the An Dun singletrack has been completed a river crossing follows that will be difficult if there has been recent rain. You'll also get wet in the fording of the Allt Garbh Gaig that follows shortly after it.

The area around Gaick lodge is surrounded by mountains and is a great place to stop a while before the run down Glen Tromie and the exit to the Sustrans route that takes you back to Dalnaspidal.

1. Car Parking near Dalnaspidal, 646733 : Set off down Sustrans track to **2. Dalnacardoch, grid ref 723703** : Cross A9 here and follow LRT up glen to **3. Exit R over moor, grid ref 717789** : a damp start leads to singletrack clinging above loch and then river crossing (sometimes impossible) followed by descent of Glen Tromie to **4. Exit L onto bridge, grid ref 780968** : 1st R over bridge through Woods of Glentromie and L turn when B970 is met, head for Kingussie and follow Sustrans to **5. Junct. With A9** : Turn off R at exit before A9 onto off-road cycle path back to start.

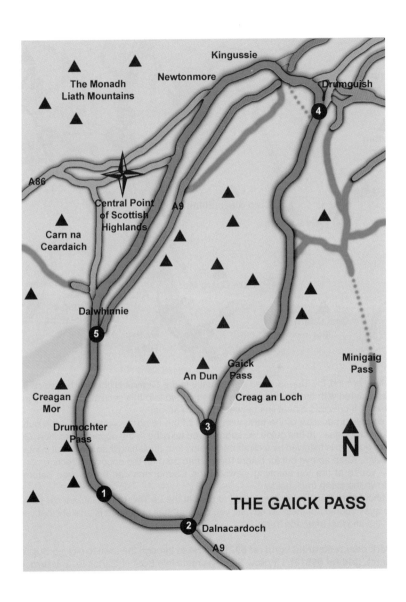

THE GAICK PASS

BURMA ROAD
Map OS Landranger Sheets 35 & 36
Distance : 44K   Ascent : 900m
Skill : Easy/Intermediate   Overall : Hard
Getting there : From S or N, A9 to Aviemore

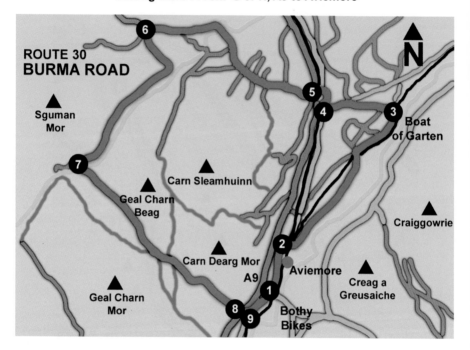

The hills around the Burma Road are actually in the Central Highlands but since it is most closely associated with the Cairngorms it's been popped into this section. However you want to look at things, it provides a neat link between the two areas.

It is so called because of the tortuous nature of the climb encountered on the outward leg when taken clockwise. In this guide we suggest you take the in the opposite direction. Going this way a slow build up is followed by a climb that seems less punishing than the brutal frontal assault from Lynwilg. Keep an eye out for bikers hammering down in the opposite direction.

Once you're at the top stunning views of the Cairngorms can be enjoyed before the big plunge down the steep track below.

You should ask permission if you want to park at the La Taverna restaurant car park. If you intend to avail yourself of their "all day, all you can eat" Italian buffet it is unlikely that you will be refused. It's an ideal after ride treat.

1. Car Park near restaurant , grid ref 892117 : Head through the town to pick up Sustrans path at **2. Junct. grid ref 896137 :** Follow Sustrans route into Boat of Garten to **3. L turn, grid ref, 943189 :** Keep with Sustrans to **4. R. turn onto B1953, grid ref 913188** : Head along to **5. L. turn from B9153, grid ref 912197 :** Cross A9 and follow LRT to rejoin Sustrans to cross Sluggan Br. to **6. L turn, grid ref. 842223 :** Head up glen to **7. Bridge, grid ref. 813166 :** Over br. & climb to descend to **8. A9, rid ref 882105 :** cross A9 then R to **9. L turn into B95152, grid ref. 881104 :** roll back to start point.

LOCH an EILEIN
Map OS Landranger Sheet 36
Distance : 16K   Ascent : 280m
Skill : Easy/Intermediate/Advanced   **Overall : Moderate**
Getting there : From S or N, A9 to Aviemore then Ski Road to Coylumbridge

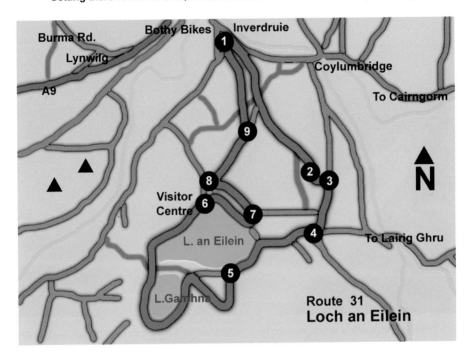

Route 31
Loch an Eilein

The relaxed atmosphere of the riding in this sheltered area makes it a good place to practice navigation skills. You can also make the riding as hard or as easy as you want.

Heading out of the Inverdruie car park along the 'Ski Road' leads to the climb onto the hill above Whitewell where views of the Rothiemurchus Forest and the surrounding hills open up before dropping to the junction where the way to the loch is signposted. Once at L. an Eilein an easy time can be enjoyed by simply following the broad track round it and L. Gamhna then heading straight for the return from near the visitor centre. Harder stuff can be found on the loch margins where you'll be presented with some stern challenges before a delightful return leg.

1. Inverdruie Car Park, grid ref 901110 : Head out of car park towards Coylumbridge to take R turn to Black Park Tullochgrue etc (signposted) until road descends to **2. Entry to path on L short of Whitewell, grid ref 916087 :** Down to **3. LRT Junct, grid ref 917087 :** Turn R and head to **4. Junct, grid ref. 916079 :** Turn R and head clockwise round loch to
5. L turn on to singletrack, grid ref, 902074 : Up climb & take 1st R branch to return to main track and follow it round L. Gamhna to take either shore of L. an Eileen (rooty & Advanced) or continue on main track to **6. Bridge, grid ref, 898084 :** Head for loch margin and follow your nose to **7. Junct. With main track, grid ref 905078 :** L along track to **8. R Turn onto private road, grid ref 897087 :** Climb over crest of hill (buildings) to **9. L turn into singletrack, grid ref. 904095 :** down through singletrack system back to car park.

LOCH EINICH
Map OS Landranger Sheet 36
Distance : 24K   Ascent : 550m
Skill : Easy/Intermediate   Overall : Moderate
Getting there : From S or N, A9 to Aviemore then Ski Road to Coylumbridge

This old favourite is a simple out and back no-brainer. As it makes its way through the Rothie-murchus forest, on a smooth surface, you'll enjoy views into the deep notch formed by the Lairig Ghru and over to Glen More.

When the track crosses the junction with the trail leading to the nearby Loch an Eilein things begin to become more interesting. The odd tree root and bare slab of rock poke through and you'll be presented with different choices of line that should be remembered for the return.

You will come to a point where the route splits and the L fork should be taken. Once clear of this section the upper glen begins to open out and a bridge is crossed (ride the ford if you dare). A deep stream crossing, with no bridge, is met higher up and can be ridden by those operating at expert level. It will normally be walking & wet feet for everyone else.

The last section to the loch is a gentle downhill that leads to the point where Am Beanaidh leaves it beneath the crags of Sgoran Dubh Mor (p78).

If the wind is absent (very rare) you'll want to linger and soak up the mountain ambience. If it is blowing strongly (more normal) it brings a welcome boost on the descent which is a carefree blast after the upper ford.

1. Car Park near Lairig Ghru Cott. , grid ref 915103 : Follow the track, keeping dead ahead and on to **2. Track end at Loch Einich, grid ref 917999 :** About turn & try to remember all the wee jumps and drops you spotted on the way up.

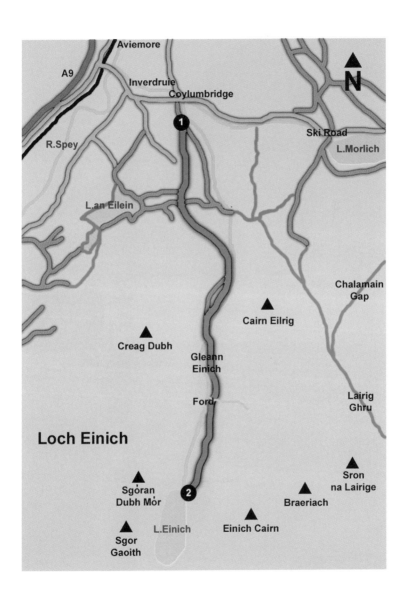

Loch Einich

Slugan singletrack

GLEN MORE
Map OS Landranger Sheet 36
Distance : 29K   Ascent : 500m
Skill : Intermediate/ Advanced   Overall : Challenging
Getting there : From S or N, A9 to Aviemore then Ski Road past Coylumbridge

This tremendous circuit provides some varied riding through Rothiemurchus and Glen More. Never too hard but with some great riding it also offers plenty of views. To keep the level at intermediate a continuation past point 6 will lead to the ski road and the option of picking up the remainder from the edge of L. Morlich.

Using the Sustrans route from Coylumbridge, it lobs off over the Slugan Pass to head for some superb singletrack (above) down to Glen More Lodge. A network of singletrack paths lies around the E end of L. Morlich that leads to its S shore and on to the last leg. This takes you to the multiple track junction known as Piccadilly. Instead of following the usual route over the Cairngorm club Footbridge this trip uses some twintrack not marked on the Landranger maps. It's great fun and ends with a fording of the R.Luineag which might be deep after rain.

There are very many variations that can be made to this route including a visit to the singletrack above the Slugan Pass (prev. page). They start off at 949127 and have some superb sections for the competent rider to explore.

1. Car Park, grid ref 932100 : L out of car park to **2. Junct with B970, grid ref 916108 :** Turn R & along road (Sustrans) to **3. Private road to Milton, grid ref 933152 :** Turn R on to LRT & keep climbing SA to descend to **4. LRT junct, grid ref 947120 :** Go L and through Badaguish to **5. Junct on L, grid ref 957113 :** take 1st L onto LRT to LRT to **6. LRT Junct, grid ref. 961111 :** Turn L and climb to cross gully and descend to **7. Junct. Grid ref 979099 :** climb to **8. ST desc. Grid ref 989102 :** Down to **9. Track at Glen More Lodge, grid ref. 988095 :** Turn L and take 1st R to follow ST to cross ski road and into more ST to cross Br to **10. LRT junct. Grid ref 970089 :** Turn R and follow LRT to **11. LRT junct grid ref. 956093:** Turn L and follow LRT to **12. Multiple track junct, grid ref. 938076:** Turn R onto Twintrack which leads to fording of river and L turn back to start.

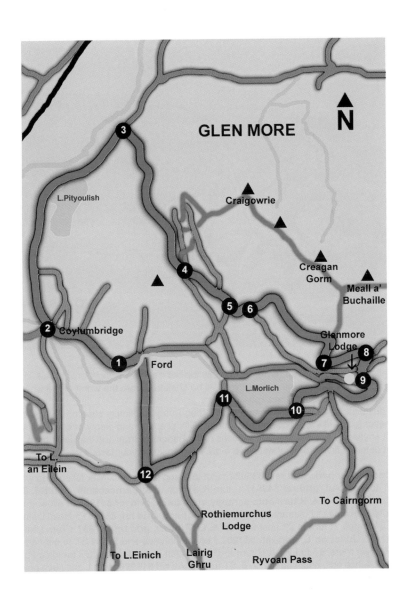

INSHRIACH
Map OS Landranger Sheet 35
Distance : 30K   Ascent : 720m
Skill : Advanced   **Overall : Challenging**
Getting there : From S or N A9 to Kingussie then B970, past Ruthven, to follow signs for
Inshriach and Uath Lochan

Attention has to be paid to navigation on this trip but it's more straightforward than the directions sound. It is a terrific outing where you will be sheltered from the worst of the weather and takes in some fabulous singletrack (p84).

The descents to Corranstilmore and from Creag Dubh are simply superb. Always demanding but never too hard they allow the exercise of skills at speed and plenty of soft landings if you overcook anything. The last leg uses sections of the Badenoch Way and the view above appears on it just before a final drop that will leave a great big smile on your face.

1. Uath lochan car park, grid ref. 835022 : Exit to S and follow track over felled area with L turn onto LRT to **2. Road, grid ref 843017 :** turn R and on to **3. Carncachuin, grid ref. 846942 :** Turn R uphill on LRT to **4. R turn onto scrappy quad track, grid ref 841955 :** Follow track dead ahead until it becomes singletrack, follow to **5. Track junct, grid ref. 833981 :** Head L along track to cross 2 bridges, R turn at 2nd past farm to **6. LRT Junct. grid ref 837997 :** Turn L into forest, continue to **7. Junct on L, grid ref. 831007 :** up into larches and follow ST to old cart chassis to turn R down more ST to LRT & R turn to Creag Dubh summit, follow ST trending R (beware barbed wire fence on L near summit) to **8. ST junct, grid ref 816996 :** turn L and keep on main ST to LRT & turn R to **9. Cairned junct, grid ref. 810001 :** descend from junct to exit & turn R along LRT that leads to ST (Badenoch Way) heading to **10. B970, grid ref. 819019 :** follow signs for Badenoch Way to **11. Junct. On R, (Badenoch Way marker) grid ref 828029:** R onto Badenoch Way and follow high track to descend back to Uath Lochan & start point.

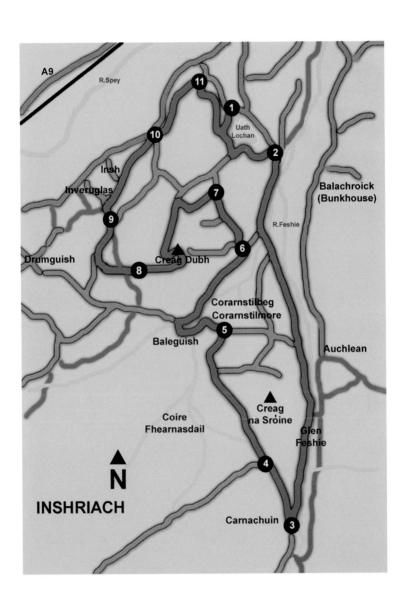

Perfection, Inshriach

Last descent of the day, Angus Glens

THE FUNGLE & MOUNTH ROADS
Map OS Landranger Sheet 44
Distance : 52K   Ascent : 1,600m
Skill : Advanced   Overall : Epic
Getting there : From S or N A90 to B966 to Edzell and follow signs for Glen Esk to car park at foot of Glen Mark

The Fungle and Mounth Roads were ancient paths linking Glens Esk and Tanar. Each traverses high passes. To get the best of the riding the circuit should be done anti-clockwise. Although there will be carrying up the Mounth Road near the end of the day it is far less than that to be endured heading S from Birse. Sometimes described as two separate trips it's far better to wait until you've built up the stamina and confidence to take on a big loop that will leave you tired but pretty chuffed with yourself.

The route is rich in singletrack and always well defined. One exception is the watershed below Tampie where the LRT peters out. The initial part of the ensuing descent is steep, lumpy, and indistinct. Here, it is best to dismount until good singletrack (a short dist. below) is found and the blast down to Birse started in earnest   Later, the singletrack leading to the Guard is one of the highlights of the day before the route heads to Glen Tanar. This passes pleasantly and leads to the intimidating prospect of the Mounth Road where steep but rideable LRT extends to the 500m contour. Just over 0.5k of carrying (for the fit) follows before the bike can be re-mounted and some interesting riding enjoyed before the big descent of the day.

The descent into Glen Mark is superb fun. For the most part, it's open and any walkers will be seen well in advance. On the sections where this is not the case you'll be slowed right down by the hairpins. Otherwise, it's a brilliant brake-burning end to a superb expedition.

1. Car park near Auchronie, Glen Mark: Head back down road to **2. Tarfside, grid ref 492797:** Follow LRT & signs for Fungle Rd. to watershed beneath Tampie and descend to **3. Junct with singletrack, grid ref 521900 :** Turn L onto singletrack and head N (shallow fords) past Birse Castle to **4. LRT continuation of Fungle, grid ref 517906 :** Climb then descend past building to look out for **5. Junct with singletrack (signposted), grid ref. 517937 :** Superb singletrack to **6. The Guard, grid ref 520955 :** Turn L and follow **7. L turn, grid ref 515957:** More LRT over N flank of Baudy Meg to descend to **8. LRT junct. grid ref, 481942 :** R & downhill to **9. Bridge over R.Tanar, grid ref. 478953 :** Over br. Turn L and head up Glen Tanar to take Mounth Road over W flank of Mt. Keen followed by descent to Glen Mark & return to start.

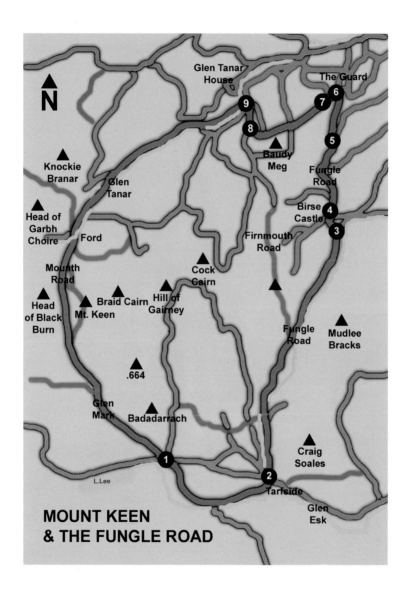

Heading up the Mounth Road

Descending Coire Chash

LOCH MUICK
Map OS Landranger Sheet 44
Distance : 25K   Ascent : 1,000m
Skill : Expert   Overall : Hard
Getting there : From S or N A90, follow signs for, then through, Kirriemuir then B955 to Glen Clova

Without a doubt this is one of the best routes in the country. This is especially so if the wee diversion up to the Dubh Loch is taken (p 67). Other than that, it's a straightforward day of two long, hard, climbs followed by two exciting descents.

Each climb and each descent has its own character and none of them takes any prisoners in the process. The descent of Corrie Chash (p 89) requires considerable expertise in the art of getting the bike off the ground and a great deal of confidence if it is to be taken at any kind of speed. The final descent is relatively smooth but it's steep, very steep and needs plenty of control.

The sweating and the adrenaline are broken up by a relaxed tour round Loch Muick; one of the most picturesque bodies of water in the country.

Every part of the day is full of mountain tops whatever direction you look. It's hard to think of any day that crams more into such a relatively compact route. Absolutely wonderful!

1. LRT entry to Glen Clova, grid ref 285761 : Head up glen and ride as close as you can to **2. Bachnagairn Bridge, grid ref 254796 :** Down to bridge and short carry up zigzags on opposite side on to high track over plateau to **3. LRT at building, grid ref 256809 :** Turn R and ride short distances to **4. L turn to Corrie Chash, grid ref 259809 :** Descend! to **5. Loch Muick, grid ref. 274818 :** Follow loch track clockwise to **6. Boat house, grid ref 295845 :** Turn R and head over bridge to turn L at LRT and on to **7. LRT junct, grid ref 305846 :** Climb, climb, climb to reach top of descent of Capel Mounth and return to start.

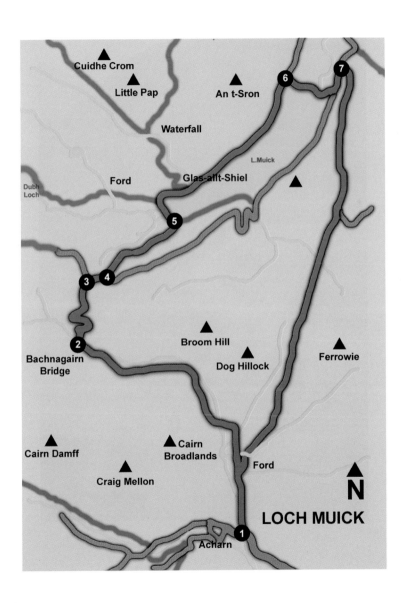

Heading for Annat

**37. Oich & Lundie, 38. Bealach an Sgairne,
39. Fionnaraich & Lair, 40. Coire Mhic Nobuil,
41. Loch na-h-Oidhche, 42. The Tollie Path,
43. Lochan Fada, 44.Loch Affric,
45. Cougie**

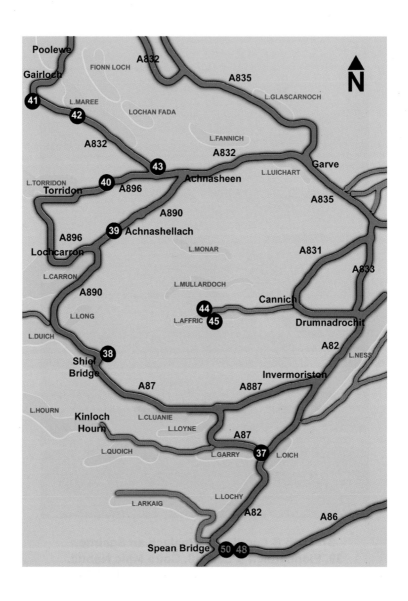

More so than any other area, much heart searching had to be done to decide what to put in and what to leave out in this region. We've provided a selection that typifies the scenery and riding within a loop from Invergarry through Kintail, Wester Ross and visiting the unmissable Glen Affric before heading back to the Great Glen.

The first offering, near the Southern end of the Great Glen, is an easy circuit that can be varied greatly as it tours Loch Oich and samples some of the singletrack in Glen Garry. The second route circumnavigates the huge bulk of Beinn Fhada in Kintail and is an altogether more serious undertaking.

From Kintail we then move to Achnashellach in Strathcarron to one of the finest routes in the country. The Fionnaraich and Lair loop (above) takes you through some unlikely territory, and into Glen Torridon, with an amazingly small amount of carrying. Again it's a day that's open to much variation but the itinerary described probably constitutes the best mix of options. The truly heroic may want to combine it with its sister route round Coire Mhic Nobuil in Torridon but the demands of that trip are quite enough for one day for most riders.

After Torridon the area round Gairloch is explored in two superb outings. The out and back to Loch na-h-Oidhche is relatively easy but tremendously rewarding. The Tollie Path is superb and brings plenty of excitement in addition to the stunning views of Loch Maree, the West coast and the many surrounding mountains. At the opposite end of Loch Maree, a hidden gem lies waiting in the shape of the Lochan Fada route. The hard work and intricate riding takes you to and from a place of outstanding beauty beneath Slioch, Scotland's loveliest mountain.

The selection ends with two tremendous routes around Glen Affric. The trip round Loch Affric itself is relatively easy and travels through magnificent landscapes with little in the way of difficulty. It can be extended towards Kintail in an out and back addition that brings some great riding. The Cougie trip takes you over to Tomich where the contrast between the rugged Highland scenery of Affiric is contrasted with the lush floor of the glen there. This is emphasised on the return which negotiates some fabulous singletrack which, itself, can be supplemented with a visit to Plodda Falls en-route. It can be added to the Loch Affric route to make a big day that will satisfy any rider.

The Great Glen and Corrieyairack three day route dips its toes into the North and provides a superb expedition. It is found in the section following this one.

LOCH OICH
Map OS Landranger Sheet 34
Distance : 28K   Ascent : 550m
Skill : Easy/ Intermediate Overall : Moderate
Getting there : From S or N, AA82 to parking near Laggan Locks

Even in the dull and drizzly evening this route was re-ridden for the book it still provided tons of fun. On that occasion we took the variation that breaks off @ 299045 (see map) to cross the moors on a mixture of twintrack and singletrack.

The way described here simply follows the LRT up to L. Lundie after the lovely easy start, along L. Oich. It is also possible to simplify the route by using the Great Glen Cycle Route to head back to Invergarry.

Apart from great views, the highlight of the trip is the singletrack along the River Garry from White Bridge. It's tremendous fun and is seldom busy with walkers. The singletrack ends at a lovely suspension bridge that will carry you over the River Garry to the Great Glen Cycle Route. This will take you back to the A82 near your start point. There is an hotel there where some well earned nosebag can be enjoyed after a cracking run.

1. Car Park beside L.Oich, grid ref 304989 : Exit L along A82, over swing bridge to **2. Turn off to water park, grid ref 300982 :** Follow road system to Great Glen Way (GGW) and along L.Oich to **3. Bridge of Oich, grid ref 339035 :** Cross suspension bridge to exit R onto LRT and follow to **4. Junct. Grid ref 335056 :** Keep straight ahead, do not turn R and follow LRT above campsite & through buildings to **5. Junct, grid ref 284022 :** Turn L and descend to **6. A87, grid ref 282018 :** Go L to **7. Entry to White Bridge car park, grid ref 285013 :** Take L onto singletrack just before bridge & follow this to **8. Suspension bridge, grid ref 301007 :** Cross and enter Great Glen Cycle Path to take you back to **9. A82, grid ref 301987 :** head L back to start point.

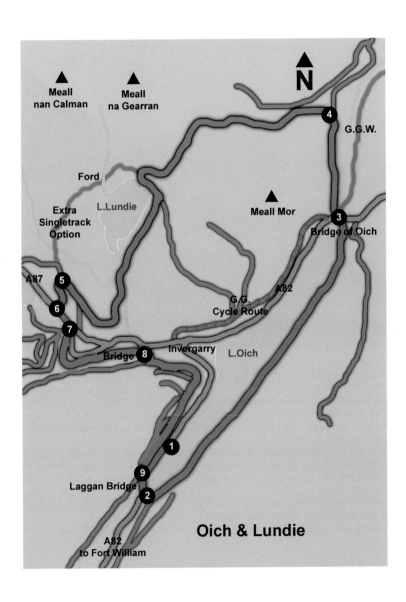

Meall
nan Calman

Meall
na Gearran

Ford

Extra
Singletrack
Option

L.Lundie

Meall Mor

G.G.W.

4

3
Bridge of Oich

A87

5

6

7

A82

G.G.
Cycle Route

Bridge

8

Invergarry

L.Oich

1

9

Laggan Bridge

2

A82
to Fort William

Oich & Lundie

BEALACH an SGAIRNE
Map OS Landranger Sheet 33
Distance : 28K   Ascent : 950m
Skill : Expert   Overall : Hard
Getting there : From S (Ft. William) A82 to Invergarry then A87 to Morvich. From N (Inverness) A82 to Invermoriston then A887 to A87 & on to Morvich

From the start of this route, great big hairy mountains crowd round you when you enter the jaws of Glen Lichd . They force you up the only way through; the precipitous path at its head. This hardship is eased by the surroundings and is over soon enough. Things open up on the descent that follows. Fun riding brilliant views are enjoyed as you head toward the turn into Gleann Gniomhaidh. Pleasant climbing is enjoyed before the steep pull up to the Bealach an Sgairne. The riding which follows is superb.

Several stream crossings that might be difficult after heavy rain will be met. You'll be wanting dry conditions anyway, the rocks round here are pretty slippery when wet. Plenty of them will need to be ridden over if you are to stay aboard the bike in the technical bits that make up the best riding.

A drop to the watercourse below beckons in the middle part of the descent. So, take care! In the lower glen the riding is less stressful but still superb.

Once things get grassy on either side the riding becomes a romp all the way back to the car park.

1. Car Park at Countryside Centre, grid ref 961211915103 : Head up Glen Lichd, with a fair bit of carrying, take care above waterfall (steep drop on R), over watershed to **2. Track junct. short of Altbeithe, grid ref 073198 :** Turn L up Gleann Gniomhaidh upt bealach an Sgairne, descent very demanding at first & care required in Gleann Choinneachan (narrow singletrack with steep drops on R), several watercourses to be forded, easing off in lower glen with superb fast riding back to start.

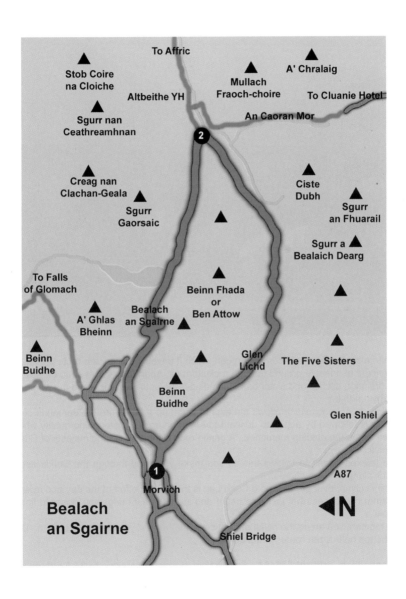

FIONNARAICH & LAIR
Map OS Landranger Sheet 25
Distance : 47K   Ascent : 1,200m
Skill : Advanced/Expert   Overall : Hard/Epic
Getting there : From S A890 vial Kintail. From N A890 via Achnasheen

Named after the two main corries through which it travels, this superb route provides a surprising amount of rideable ground through rocky terrain. Apart from the need to be able to jump and hop drainage ditches and water bars, the riding is never too technical and the whole day has a lovely rhythm to it.

Starting at Achnashellach allows the legs to warm up a bit before the demands of the first climb. This is followed by a superb descent to Annat on trails of astounding quality where rock and water will be the abiding memories. A gentle road climb through the majesty of Glen   Torridon is next.

More relaxed pedalling follows this as you make your way through the Coulin estate with singletrack along the loch shores.

The final climb, over the Drochaid Coire Lair is the last big effort of the day and rewards you with an amazing descent that just gets better and steeper as it brings you closer to floor of the glen below.

One moment you are in the midst of frantic action, the next you are at the bottom. Definitley among the top half-dozen routes in the country.

1. Achnashellach, grid ref 005484 : Follow road over level crossing to **2. Coulags, grid ref 958451 :** Head up through Coire Fionnraich then down (singletrack all the way) to **3. Annat, grid ref 894544 :** Turn R to head up glen Torridon to **4. R turn into Coulin Estate, grid ref 002582 :** Follow LRT to **5. Break off on R to Loch Coulin, grid ref. 008559 :** Descend to follow singletrack along loch and head toward Coulin Pass to **6. Junct. Grid ref 023532 :** Turn R and head over into Coire Lair for singletrack descent to Achnashellach.

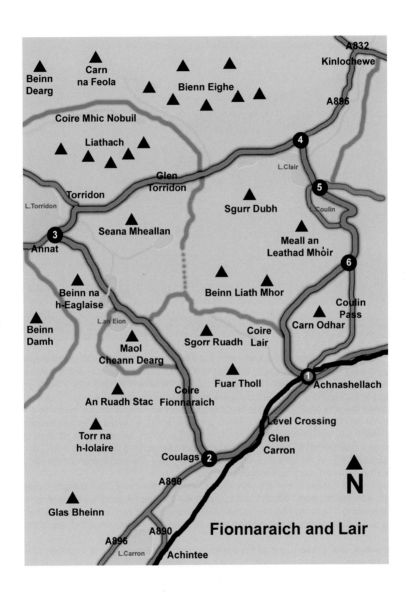

Fionnaraich and Lair

Coire Mhic Nobuil
Maps OS Landranger Sheets 24 & 25
Distance : 24K   Ascent : 600m
Skill : Expert   Overall : Hard
Getting there : From S or N A896 vial Lochcarron and Kinlochewe respectively

This is an awesome part of the world and you'll be riding through one of its most spectacular aspects. An easy start on road down Glen Torridon to the loch of the same name leads to a signposted path to Coire Mhic Nobuil. This heads up an entertaining climb through Scots pines and into the upper part of the coire. Here skills are tested on rocks and roots.

Gradually the way ahead becomes tougher and tougher. Demands are made on concentration as much as on skill and strength. There comes a point, no matter how focussed or strong you are, where you will have to dismount. The on/off sections become more off than on. Then, just when you lose the will to live and think it can't get any worse it does.

So, why bother? In the dark moments, look around you, the peaks and corries are astounding. Keep the faith and you'll be rewarded.

Suddenly it all eases off and the way ahead, down Coire Dubh Mor, stretches over 4k and 300m right into the car park. Starting off fast and easy angled it splashes through a few burns before steepening. Tight zig-zags on immaculately constructed cobbled sections follow that test cornering skill. Awkwardly placed ditches to be hopped, jumped or wheelied, add further interest.

It's a skilled rider's dream and all the earlier cursing and floundering is forgotten within about a minute. Honest.

1. Car Park Glen Torridon, grid ref 958568 : Down glen to **2. Junction, grid ref 906557 :** Head for Alligin, up steep road climb to **3. Signpost for Coire Mhic Nobuil path, grid ref 870577 :** Turn R up path & climb as much as you can, lot of carrying between Lochan a Chaorainnn Lochan a Choire Dubh, descend to start point.

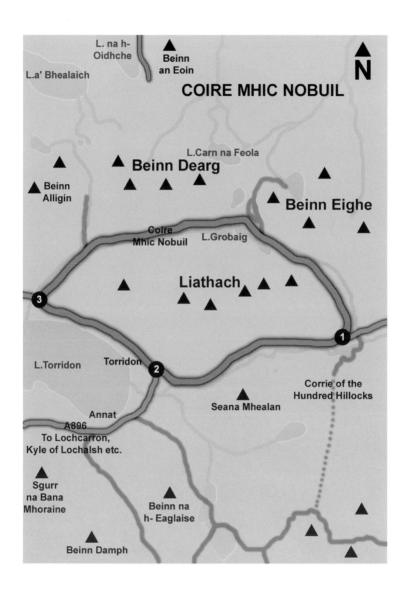

Bealach a' Choire Ghairbh

Slioch

LOCH na-h-OIDHCHE
Map OS Landranger Sheet 19
Distance : 20K   Ascent : 570m
Skill : Intermediate   Overall : Challenging
Getting there : From S A9 to Inverness then A835 to Garve followed by A832 through Kinlochewe, from N A832

Although it's not the singletrack the map seems to promise, this is a superb foray into truly wild country. It starts as reasonably smooth LRT until the first climb is completed. The rough twintrack that makes up the remainder is fabulous.

Excellent riding tests climbing skill and stamina on the outward leg and provides loads of fun on the way back. Just to make sure you are kept on your toes, there's a water splash through the Abhainn Loch na- h-Oidhche.

All the time the view changes and the peaks on the N side of Loch Maree appear on the final climb to Loch na h - Oicdhche (above). When the loch is reached you are treated to an amazing view of the hills around it. Along the side of the loch the track roughens and gives enjoyable riding as it takes you up for a closer look at the back end of the Torridon peaks.

The descent is just great fun and a variation can be made by returning via Loch Bad an Sgalaig. The start to this variant is easily found by consulting the info board at the car park and is worth it just to see the waterfall it passes. The riding is none too shabby either.

1. Am Feur Loch Car Park, grid ref 857721 : Cross road from car park to enter LRT and follow to
2. Track end near Poca Buidhe bothy, grid ref 900640 : About turn & enjoy the ride.

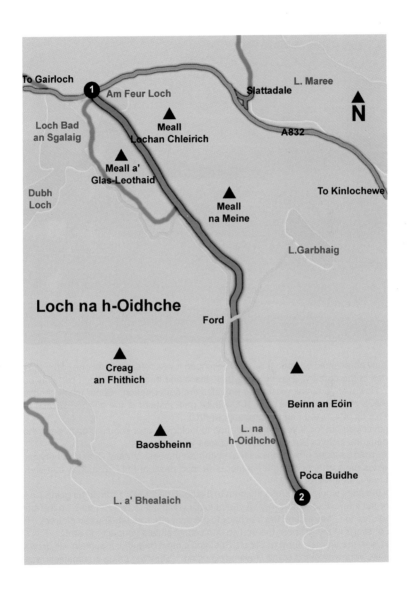

THE TOLLIE PATH
Map OS Landranger Sheet 25
Distance : 27K   Ascent : 900m
Skill : Advanced/Expert   Overall : Challenging/Hard
Getting there : From S A890 vial Kintail then A832. N (or Inverness) A835 then A832

The only other time I've seen this route described it was referred to as one of the best out and back routes in the country. Having done the " there and back again" it can certainly be recommended. However, a circuit exists and provides the better option. Some might choose to stick with the A832 all the way to the start of the Tollie path instead of the off road section described below. It's a bit of a mixed bag but probably worth it.

Whatever you opt for, if you take your time to look over your shoulder once past the Bad an Sgalaig dam, the sight of Baosbheinn will impress you.

All the road sections provide views that epitomise the best of West Coast scenery and ensure that the miles pass without being tiresome. The road descent to L. Tollaidh is fast and leads to the meat in the sandwich.

From the point where you cross the burn to the bealach there's 180m to be gained in 2.5k. It's hard work but interesting all the way. If you're lucky you'll get to see climbers on the crags. The climb, the drop to L. Maree and the trail back to the car park is all fabulous singletrack. There are a couple of stings in the tail near the end so don't congratulate yourself too early.

If it's clear, the shapely form of Slioch, Scotland's most beautiful mountain will draw your eye as you make your way along some challenging riding.   Stunning riding in a majestic setting!

1. Car park at Slattadale, grid ref 888721 : Exit car park & head straight up LRT to roA832 & turn L, along road to **2. Exit on R, opposL. Bad an Sgalaig Dam, grid ref 847721** : Follow track/path system down to **3. A832, Charlestown** : Turn R to head up road, through Gairloch and up past L.Tollaidh to **4. Entry to The Tollie Path grid ref 859790** : Follow path over bealach and down to L. Maree and back to Slattadale . Watch out for the ditches!

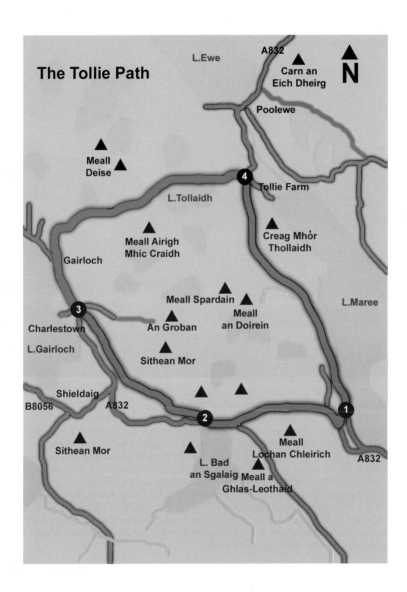

The Tollie Path

LOCHAN FADA
Map OS Landranger Sheet 19
Distance : 22K   Ascent : 700m
Skill : Advanced   Overall : Hard
Getting there : From S A9 to Inverness then A835 to Garve or A896 from Torridon
From N A832

At only 22k, this route might be regarded as a pushover by many folk. When half of it is climbing and more than half of it singletrack it should give a little pause for thought.

This journey begins gently enough by following the smooth LRT from Incheril out to where it branches off into Gleann na Muice above the Heights of Kinlochewe. A punishing climb follows up the glen to the point where the vehicle track ends and the singletrack begins (above). Slioch peeps over the hills to your L and an astounding sight awaits you when you reach Lochan Fada itself. It's another of those special places where everything seems just right.

Make your way through two big fords (and a few smaller ones) that lie between you and the struggle to the delights of Gleann Banasdail. This spectacular rift is wild and scenic. Look out for the crags and waterfall on your L at the bottom. It also makes a great descent back to Loch Maree and more singletrack back to the car park. It's a brilliant trip for those who can handle a bike, love their mountains, and enjoy hard work.

1. Incheril Car Park, grid ref. 038624 : Head up to Gleann na Muice, turning L at Heights of Kinlochewe, negotiate deer gate and climb glen to **2. Start of singletrack, grid ref. 070667 :** Follow singletrack to ford at Lochan Fada followed by 2nd ford (minor splashes in between) before beginning ascent to head of Gleann Banasdail, descend glen to **3. L turn, grid ref. 012657 :** Over bridge to follow singletrack back to start.

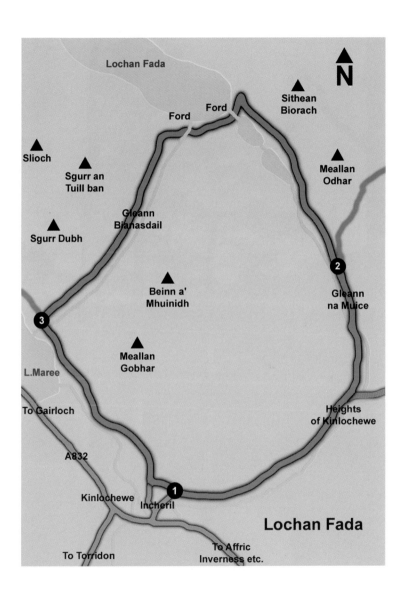

Scots Pines, Affric

Map OS Landranger Sheet 25
Distance : 17K   Ascent : 400m
Skill : Intermediate   Overall : Moderate/Challenging
Getting there : From S or N, A82 (L.Ness) to Drumnadrochit then A831 to Cannich

The scenery here is peerless. In this easy to follow circuit you have the chance to soak up the views on the outward leg while riding a smooth, hard packed LRT that is known to the survivors of the Highland Cross as" the Yellow Brick Road." "The Cross" is an annual duathlon in which the victims run from Kintail to jump on their bikes near the Glen Affic roadhead before cycling into Beauly. By the time the poor souls reach Athnamulloch their legs are tired and the hard surface of the LRT you will be riding is met. For many every step is torture. Hence the wry nickname. With fresh legs and a spring in your pedal stroke it's a doddle.

Your own real work begins after crossing the Allt na Ciche about half way out. After the bridge, the track rears up and a stiff climb follows to take you to the rough twintrack that leads back along the N side of L. Affric.   It's enormously entertaining and peppered with muck, rock and water splashes. One or two of the burns may pose problems if there has been heavy rainfall. The remainder of the track offers plenty of options allowing the grade to be kept at a modest Intermediate if the stream crossings are paddled through. Fabulous.

1. Car Park near at W end of L. Beinn a Mheadhoin, 201234 : Cross bridge below car park and head R on well surfaced LRT (the Yellow Brick Road) to **2. Junct. , grid ref 138206 :** Turn R and head past buildings , main track ford, singletrack to R plank bridge, cross bridge over Allt na Ciche, up steep climb to **3. Junction, grid ref 120208 (do not use steep shortcut up bank, stay on main track until proper junction reached!)** Turn R and head back to start with loads of fun along the way.

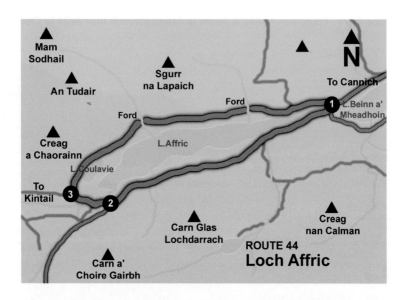

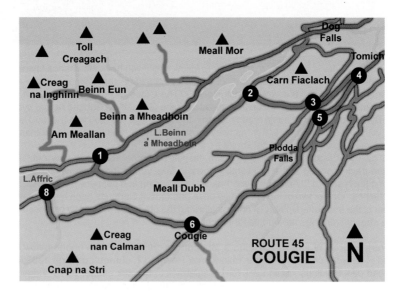

COUGIE

Map OS Landranger Sheet 25
Distance : 33K   Ascent : 750m
Skill : Advanced   **Overall : Challenging**
Getting there : From S or N, A82 (L.Ness) to Drumnadrochit then A831 to Cannich

The Cougie round is a fine partner to the Yellow Brick Road circuit. Doing both in a day is a good test of strength and endurance but each more than justifies a separate outing. The variety provided by this day is sufficient reason for it to be savoured on its own.

Beginning from the road end car park at the head of L. Beinn a' Mheadhoin (pronounced vane) the bridge is crossed to head E along the banks of the loch. The Scots pines here are majestic and a reminder of how things once were. The trees are sufficiently open to allow the scenery on the far side of the loch to be enjoyed. A climb then a swoop down to Tomich follows.

At the bottom the scenery changes into a lush valley that is far removed from the wild Highland Glen behind you. A roll along the glen floor, followed by a climb past the Plodda Falls (a look at the map shows a loop that's worth the extra effort), takes you up beyond Cougie to a point where everything dwindles into singletrack.

A stunning panorama lies ahead. The riding is great too and the narrow track entertains before finishing abruptly near the start. Pick dry conditions to avoid damage and to get the best of it.

1. Car Park at head of L. Beinn a' Mheadhoin, grid ref 200233 : Cross Br. & turn L, head along loch side track to **2. Junct. grid ref 254261:** Climb & descend to **3. Junct, grid ref 286258 :** down hairpin and L at bottom to head to **4. Road , grid ref 304269 :** head up glen and into estate road track system to **5. Junct at ruin, grid ref 288253 :** Turn R and follow track, trending L at fork & climb past Plodda path entry continuing dead ahead to **6. Cougie, grid ref 241211 :** straight ahead until singletrack reached and descent to **7. Junct. With LRT, grid ref 181224 :** turn R and head down to start.

Loafers

46. Loch Tay Loop,
47. Loch Etive & Glen Kinglass,
48. Leanachan, Leven, Luibeilt, Leacach,
49. Gaick & Feshie, 50. The Great Glen & the Corrieyairack

The notion of cycle touring appeals to most riders. The idea of rolling off into the distance, carrying all you need on the bike, is something most of us have thought about or done at one time or another. On straightforward road cycling trips it's a simple matter of sticking some panniers to the frame, loading the bike up, and off we go. Oh that it could be so simple with a mountainbike tour.

A laden bike is slow and difficult to manoeuvre on technical ground. It's murder to lift over gates or coax over obstacles like the bridge seen above. Moving all the weight into a big rucksack isn't the answer either. The riders on this page and the previous one were heading in for a weekend's riding based at a bothy. The track into it wasn't at all technical and the destination not that far from the roadhead. So, they loaded up with grub and coal and struggled in.

For proper mountain biking a heavy load on the shoulders impedes balance and breathing. Using a trailer is one solution but it will still be a nuisance over the same stuff that panniers cause the grief on. Also, they're so big you usually end up taking too much stuff.

If you are determined to be totally self-sufficient and carry a tent, stoves, food and all the necessary comforts then a compromise will have to be made. Some of us think it's far better to travel light and stay fast.

If you are willing to stay at hotels, B&Bs or bunkhouses then possibilities begin to open up a little bit more. By keeping weight to a minimum, and the bike unfettered, mobility is maintained and technical ground can be tackled. This approach allows for far more interesting tours to be undertaken. With a meal and bed waiting at the end of a day all that need be carried for the overnight stay is a lightweight pair of trousers, shirt, underwear and sandals. This can be supplemented by the normal emergency clothing that you would carry on any trip. Your pack need weigh no more than 1.5-2kilos heavier than on an ordinary day's riding. This is the way many choose to conduct their tours and how it is suggested you follow those included here.

If you've not done such things before it's best to get some practice in by riding long routes two days in a row. This will increase your fitness and let you get an idea of how your body reacts to the demands without the pressure of completing an actual tour.

One thing which is an absolute prerequisite on multi-day cycling is hygiene. You must wear a fresh pair of riding shorts each day and keep your own contact points scrupulously clean. If you don't you'll eventually fall foul of saddle sores. Get them once and you'll know!

The five tours featured are all designed to be ridden in the hit and run style. They're all fairly long and have varying degrees of difficulty but each provides a satisfying mixture of challenge and reward worthy of anybody's attention.

LOCH TAY LOOP

Map OS Landranger Sheet 57, 51,52
Distance : 130k Ascent : 2,900m
Day 1 64K -1,400m   Day 2 66k - 1,500
Skills : Easy/Intermediate   Overall : Hard
Getting there : From N or S A9 to Perth then A85 through Crieff to Comrie

The big distances on this tour are easily broken up with pit stops at the many hotels and tea rooms encountered along the way.

Day one begins with a gentle amble along the road up Glen Artney before LRT is met at it's end. This will take you below Ben Vorlich and down into Callander where tea rooms abound. The Sustrans track is then taken through Balquhidder where another stop can be made at the tea room above. The Sustrans track continues spectacularly up Glen Ogle before depositing you at Killin where there are plenty of places to stay including the youth hostel.

Day two follows the S shore of L.Tay before cutting off through the impressive cleft of Gleann Chilleine and into Glen Ample. The road through the Sma' Glen is taken to a turn off that leads up on to a high track from which Lowland Perthshire can be surveyed before reaching the final turn that plunges you back to Comrie.

A look at the maps will show that several variations. The most obvious allow extra singletrack to be included in Glen Artney, in the descents to Callander or the inclusion of Glen Ample. They may make combinations that will be more appealing to the advanced riders.

1st DAY   1. Car park at East end of Comrie, grid ref. 777223 : Turn R through town & take B827 into Glen Artney and follow to LRT continuation past Arivurichardich and on to Callander, turning R along A84 into town & L at junct with A81 to **2. Entry to Sustrans route, grid ref. 627079 :** follow Sustrans route all the way to **3. Junct with A827 Killin, grid ref 572324:** Locate accommodation.

2nd DAY return to 3. head E along Sustrans route on S shore of L.Tay to **4. Ardtalnaig & turn off to LRT, grid ref. 702392 :** Head up Gleann a Chilleine with ST link to Glen Almond and on to **5. Newton br, grid ref: 888316 :** Turn R along A822 & along Sma' glen past hotel to **6. Exit on R to LRT, grid ref 890262:** Climb up LRT to high track heading W to pass Turret Dam and continuation of LRT on W to **7. LRT junct, grid ref 797256:** descend to Comrie.

120

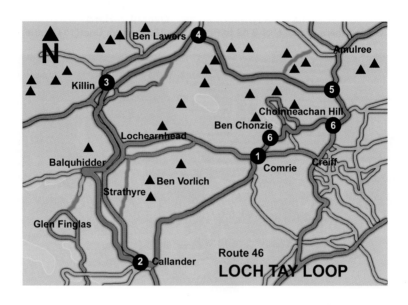

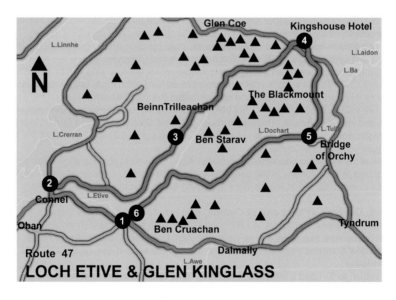

LOCH ETIVE & GLEN KINGLASS

Map OS Landranger Sheet 50,41
Distance : 114k Ascent : 2,500m
Day 1 64K -1,500m   Day 2 50k - 1,000m
Skills : Intermediate/Advanced   Overall : Hard/Epic
Getting there : From S A82 to Tyndrum then A85 to Taynuilt, From N (Ft.William) A82 to Ballachulish then A828 to Connel followed by A85 to Taynuilt

Each of the two days in this trip has totally different characters. For one thing, there is not much in the way of downhill action on day one. However, the scenery enjoyed more than makes up for this. If you're lucky the Falls of Lora will be in full flow beneath the Connell Bridge as L. Awe empties it's contents into L. Linnhe. Once the derelict buildings and quarry at Bonawe are passed things become wilder and the views more breathtaking as Ben Starav and Ben Trilleachan compete for your attention on opposite sides of the loch.

When the head of the loch is reached, after passing through beautiful woodland, the long pull up Glen Etive is crowded with glimpses into corries and to the high tops that surround it. Once at your night's stopover the same peaks can be enjoyed from the twin comforts of an armchair and a full stomach.

Day two begins with a climb that might be hard on the legs after the previous day's exertions but the sights of the Buchaille Etive Mor and Rannoch Moor will ease the pain until the first descent to Ba Bridge and its spectacular rock formations. When Victoria Bridge is reached it is a small matter to roll the few K to Inveroran if a break is needed prior to heading for Glen Kinglass.

Before the watershed into Kinglass is crossed you will pass L. Dochart and its brethren and marvel at the peaks about you. Once the ensuing rock slabs and suspension bridge is negotiated you will be able to enjoy a great descent, with rocky bits, until another bridge is met.

LRT lies beyond and the remainder of the glen is smooth and easy-angled enough to allow the views to be savoured. On hot days few will be able to resist a bit of skinny dipping in one of the pools in the river.

At the foot of the glen a little more work lies ahead to get you back to the start.

1st DAY 1. Taynuilt Stn. : Head W along the B8079 and follow it to Connel to cross the bridge to **2. R turn onto minor road, grid ref 911348 :** Follow road to Bonawe where it becomes LRT and keep SA to **3. LRT junct, grid ref. 056388 :** Turn L and climb & keep SA to head of loch where road is met, follow road up glen and cross A82 **4. Kingshouse Hotel, grid ref, 259547**
2nd Day 4. Kingshouse Hotel : From hotel head up remnants of old road to cross A82 toward White corries Ski station, turning L on to West Highland Way & follow this to **5. Victoria Bridge, grid ref 271423 :** Turn R and head down Glen Kinglass then S along L. Etive to road & turn R to roll along to **6. L turn to footbridge, grid ref 021317:** Over footbridge & turn R to reach Taynuilt

LEANACHAN , LEVEN, LUIBEILT & LEACACH LOOP
Map OS Landranger Sheet 41
Distance : 90K Ascent : 2,700m
Skills : Advanced Overall : Hard
Getting there : Train ; Spean Bridge Stn. Road ; from S A82 (Fort William).
From E A9 via Dalwhinnie or Newtonmore then A86

An awesome tour for the fit, committed and skilled rider! Starting at Spean Bridge railway station it begins gently enough on its journey to Fort William. The West Highland Way (WHW) is then followed, with plenty of singletrack action, and a steep descent, to Kinlocheven for your overnight stop.

Day two begins with an ascent past the Mamore Lodge Hotel and on to the stunning open area around Loch Eilde Mor. The crescendo comes after the sometimes difficult river crossing at Luibeilt and the tough climbing to the bealach above the Lairig Leacach. The memory of the singletrack descent that follows will live with you a long time. After that it's a simple matter of heading N along the LRT to the road that leads to the start.

There are several ways to vary this trip. On day one, a diversion to the delights of the Witch's Trails only adds a couple of K. If you're feeling very energetic a way exists that takes you up to the foot of the Northern corries of Ben Nevis before dropping to the Aluminium works.

On day two it's possible to make your way up to the Blackwater dam and traverse the path beside the aqueduct to take you to the Eilde lochs. It's also a simple matter to squeeze some extra, easy, singletrack in at the end by diverting into the Leanacahan Forest.

Have a good look at the map and see what suits you best, they're all good.

1ˢᵗ DAY **1. Spean Bridge Stn. :** Head E along A82 to **2. L turn onto minor road , grid ref 208812 :** Under railway & 1ˢᵗ R to parallel railway on LRT, crossing Nevis range access road & through Torlundy to **3. R turn onto path, grid ref. 146763:** Follow this past aluminium works onto A82 & signs for Glen Nevis to **4. Entry to LRT (WHW) on R, grid ref 122737 :** follow LRT and signs for WHW (walkers, take care!) all the way to Kinlochleven

2ⁿᵈ Day **5. Access road to Mamore Lodge Hotel, grid ref. 176623 :** Climb past hotel and on past Eilde Mor etc **6. Luibeilt & river crossing near, grid ref 263685 :** Crossing sometimes dangerous! Over river to climb & carry to bealach & ST descent to **7. LRT junct. Near Leacach Bothy, grid ref 283738 :** Turn L and head back to start on LRT then road.

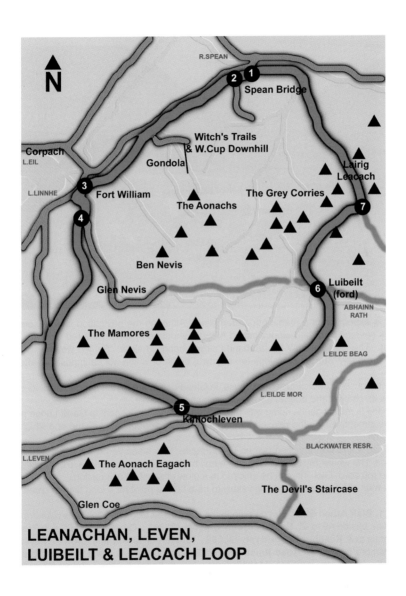

**LEANACHAN, LEVEN,
LUIBEILT & LEACACH LOOP**

GAICK & FESHIE LOOP
Map OS Landranger Sheet 42, 35,36,43
Distance : 124K Ascent : 2,500m
Day 1 66K -1,200m   Day 2 58k - 1,300m
Skills : EXPERT   Overall : Epic+
Getting there : Train ; Blair Atholl Stn. Road ; from S or N A9 to Blair Atholl

This is expedition is a mammoth undertaking. Although the navigation is pretty simple the distances covered and the height climbed mean it should only be considered by the fittest and strongest. The riding on day two demands strong handling skills. Settled weather is required as there are many stream crossings (on day two) some of which will be impossible after heavy rain.

March House or Balachroick bunkhouse, in Glen Feshie, are recommended as places to stay. Each has its charms and budget may decide which you choose.

Day one is mainly gentle riding with the An Dun ST and the descent to Gaick Lodge providing some excitement. Enjoy the relaxed atmosphere and pace of this day as the one which follows is a monster.

Day two starts with the long pull up Glen Feshie. This takes you deep into the heart of the mountains. The whole day is rich in ST with many hard and intricate sections to be dealt with after which the roll down Glen Tilt can be enjoyed in a glow of satisfied exhaustion.

It's a tour with few equals and one likely to be a talking point for a long time to come.

1st DAY 1. Blair Atholl Stn. : Head W along the B8079 and follow the Sustrans markers to traffic free section beside A9 to **2. Dalnacardoch grid ref 723703 :** Cross A9, over Gaick Pass & own Glen Tromie to **3. Killiehuntly, grid ref. 790988 :** Turn R & on to LRT and follow LRT system past Corranstilmore farm to **4. Road junct, grid ref 840000 :** Turn L & along TM to **5. R turn onto RoW to Feshiebridge, grid ref. 844015:** Follow it to **6. Feshiebridge :** Take LRT on opposite side of river that leads to Glen Feshie and Balachroick bunkhouse.

2nd Day 7. Balachroick Bunkouse, grid ref 850009 : Follow your front wheel up Glen Feshie and over watershed into Glen Geldie to **8. Junct, grid ref 005868 :** Turn R (S) past Bynack and cross watershed into Glen Tilt and homeward leg down the glen.

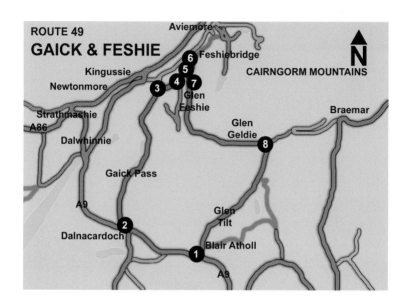

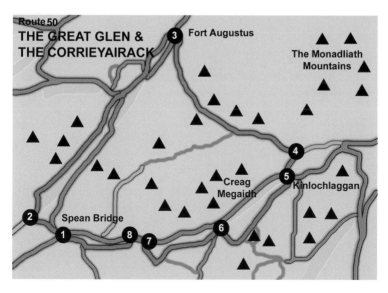

Towpath, approaching Br. of Oich

THE GREAT GLEN & THE CORRIEYAIRACK PASS

Map OS Landranger Sheet 50,41
Distance : 128k Ascent : 2,670m
Day 1 45K -780m   Day 2 36k - 1,130m Day 3 47k - 760m
Skills : Intermediate Overall : Epic
Getting there : Train ; Spean Bridge Stn. Road ; from S A82 (Fort William).
From E A9 via Dalwhinnie or Newtonmore then A86

This three day expedition is a superb trip that really has a bit of everything.

Day 1 is straightforward enough and simply follows the Great glen Cycleway from Gairlochy to Fort Augustus. It's not quite the pushover you might think and you should take it easy to save some energy for the second day.

Day 2 starts with a the mammoth haul up and over the Corrieyairack. Once at the summit the descent is a real screamer and leads to the second overnight stop at Kinloch Laggan.

Day 3 leads through the Ardverikie estate, past Lochan na-h-Earba through beautiful sur-roundings. At Luiblea the choice can be made to follow the standard route by turning R or you can make your way up to 402740 to see Strath Ossian and tackle the tough link to Fersit.

As you cross the FB at Monessie it's worthwhile leaving the bikes on the far side and taking a walk downriver to see the spectacular gorge there. After that it's a simple matter to follow the LRT until it becomes the road that leads back to the start.

1st DAY 1. Spean Br. Stn. : Follow signs for A82 N and turn off at Commando memorial to descend to Gairlochy and follow Great Glen Cycleway all the way to Fort Augustus.
2nd Day 2. Fort Augustus : Make your way out along B862 to **3. R turn onto minor road, grid ref 386084 :** Head along to 3. L Turn into Corrieyairack, grid ref. 373072 Climb pass and descend to **4. L turn onto LRT, grid ref 553932:** Follow LRT to Kinloch Laggan.
3rd Day Kinloch Laggan: Make your way to **5. Access road to Ardverikie Est. grid ref. 539897:** Over Br & 1st R to **6. LRT junct. Grid ref 509874 :** climb and ride alongside Lochan na-h-Earba to **7. LRT Junct. Luiblea, Grid ref. 434828:** Turn L and follow LRT SA through Fersit and on to **8. A86, grid ref. 341809:** Turn L and continue to **9. L turn to Monessie Gorge, grid ref. 302810:** Descend & cross FB over waterfall, follow LRT back to minor road and on to Spean Br.